Becoming the
One Percenter

How You Can Become the
Best of the Best

By

Kimberly Peters

Disclaimer

This publication is intended as a resource to help people achieve more and lead happier lives. Since everyone is different and every situation is different, there is no way to create one perfect plan or approach to anything in life. Therefore the information within this book should not be used as a specific plan or approach by any individual. It is the sole responsibility of the individual to choose which information is practical and applicable to their own situation. The publishers, writers and distributors of this publication assume no responsibility or liability for the use or application of any or all parts of this publication.

Table of Contents

Introduction

Do you have what it takes to be among the best? Do you have a desire to be among the best at anything in your life? That's a question many of us never really think about. After all, you don't have to be the best at something to succeed in life. There are many people who appear to do just fine following what others have done and never really doing anything special.

Success is something that everyone seems to have a different view or perception about. For some people, success means earning more money than anyone else. For others success might mean doing things for others or doing something that makes a difference in someone else's life.

Regardless of what success might mean to you, one thing is clear. If you want to be successful at anything, you have to make a commitment to it and know what needs to be done and how to do it. Very few people get to be successful by accident.

You have to do something, have a great idea or at least start the ball rolling. Even the person who won the lottery had to go out and buy the damned ticket!

The good news for a lot of us is that it might not be all that difficult to be among the best at whatever we do in life. That is not because we are so smart, so good looking and so impressive. Far from it. It is because so many people in this world set the bar so low that it makes it easy for people like you and I to rise to the top.

The most successful people in this world are not always the smartest or the best looking. They are the ones who were not afraid to do those things others refuse to do. These are the people who were not afraid to take that first step while others might have let fear get the best of them. Most important, these are the people who knew what they wanted out of life and figured out how to go about getting it.

At the end of the day, success should be doing what you want to in life while being able to avoid the things you don't like. It is about feeling good when you wake up and pleased with how the day went when you go to sleep at night. Life is about choices and those who are at the top get the most options in life.

So right now we have a choice to make. If you want to be at the top, if you want to be a "one percenter" then you need to throw out some of the ideals and opinions you already have and agreed to open your mind just a little bit. This isn't going to be hard and it isn't going to be painful. But it is going to take more effort than laying on the beach on a sunny afternoon. But one thing remains very clear. If you are willing to do some things right now, there will be a lot more opportunities to lay on that beach on a sunny afternoon in your future.

Before we get started, let's talk a little bit about how this book is designed and laid out. This will help you get the best results in the least amount of time.

Over the years we have learned one important thing. People who buy this type of book usually have a specific or even urgent need and because of that, they don't start at the beginning of the book. They turn to a specific chapter or section. Unfortunately, with some books, jumping ahead like that will cause you to miss some information that might make it difficult to understand something that appears later in the book.

We solved that problem by creating each and every chapter as a "stand alone" chapter which means that everything you need to understand what is in that chapter is contained in that particular chapter. So you can read a chapter, fully understand the content, and then move on.

Sometimes this means that some content might be repeated throughout the book. This is not a mistake or a way to increase page count. Instead we do this for two reasons. The first reason is what we just explained and the second reason is that usually this content is relevant and important to multiple sections in the book and repetition will help you retain the information longer.

Everything in this book, from the words used and the format chosen was designed with two things in mind. That is to give you the information you need to succeed and to get you the results you want in the fastest period of time possible. We believe we have succeeded in achieving both those goals in this book.

So here is the best way to get started. If you have a specific or urgent need, feel free to jump ahead to that section of the book. Then, once you have read that chapter and addressed that particular need, then go back and read the book from cover to cover. It isn't that long and the flow of information will help you learn even more and reinforce what you had already read even more.

Then, go out and put the information to use! Even the most powerful information will do you no good if you never apply it or use it! Take one thing at a time and adapt it to your own situation and life. Not everything may apply and some things you are probably doing already.

But still read about them to see if you can learn even more. Everyone can always learn something new every day!

So, if you're ready, let's start learning how to be one of the "One Percenters"!

Why Should You Become a One Percenter?

You are reading this book for a reason. Obviously there is an interest in making your life or yourself better in some way. But do you really know what that reason is? Do you know what is missing or what is not exactly how you would like it to be? Sometimes the answers are right in front of us and sometimes they require a bit of digging and introspection. Whatever your situation might be, you should understand it before you try and move on.

Understanding is important because the one percenters in this world all have one thing pretty much in common. That one thing is that they know what they want and they know what they need to do in order to get it.

They make fewer mistakes and they think things through.

This is important because no matter who you are; you have just so much time on this planet and no one knows in advance how much time we really have. So we need to make every effort to make sure we are heading in the right direction. That direction is towards what we want in life and where our goals are.

This will require some effort on your part but that effort will produce greater results for you and save you time and effort in the future. So what you do now will pay dividends for you later. It's like having to walk one mile to the east. If you start off walking west for a half mile, you will have to turn around and walk that same half mile back just to get to where you were when you started. |So you walked the same mile but really didn't get anywhere.

Some of you might ask "Why should I walk that mile in the first place? I'm happy enough right now."

That's a great question. The reason we should strive to be a one percenter is because we should always want the best in life for ourselves, our family and others who are important in our lives. We might be happy now but there might be little things we can do to make life even better!

As we said, the one percenters in life usually get to do more of what they like in life and less of what they dislike. You can be happy with splitting likes and dislikes 50-50 but you would be much happier with an 80-20 or even 90-10 split, right? So the point of becoming a one percenter is to live the life you WANT not the life you HAVE to live.

There's a big difference between the two. When you do the things you want to do, time goes faster, you are happier and most of the time the results are much better. When you do those things you have to do, you tend to rush through them, time drags, you tolerate things and your productivity and overall happiness is far less.

It's like the difference between liking a peanut butter sandwich and having to eat them every day because that is all you can afford! You might like them but you might like to have a steak or a nice Italian meal sometime as well. Life is nicer and more rewarding when you have more choices.

Throughout this book we are going to show you what you need to do in order to get more out of your life. More happiness, more control and more satisfaction out of your life. But you will not be successful if you don't understand why you should make the effort. Doing something for the sake of doing it usually does not end all that well. But when we understand why we should do something, that's when our results and performance go way up.

So tell yourself you want more control and more happiness in your life. Even if you are happy now, convince yourself that there is more out there for you. More to add to your life. More that will bring you satisfaction and fulfillment. But perhaps more than anything else, convince yourself that there are things that you can do to give you more choices in life.

Because when someone has more choices, they usually use those choices to do more of what they like and leave all the other stuff for others to do. Right there, that's a ton of incentive for anyone!

The One Percenter Attitude

Sometimes the difference between the successful person and the rest of us lies in their attitude. One percenters have an overwhelmingly positive attitude even when they are faced with a negative situation or even failure. One percenters also have the attitude that everything can always be made better or done differently. They are not constrained by what others always have done in the past.

One percenters believe in themselves and their abilities. They respond to most everything with a positive outlook. They try things and are not discouraged by defeat. Instead, they learn from it so that the next time they find themselves in the same situation they will be better prepared. They feel that even failure is not failure if you emerge from it smarter and better prepared for next time!

Contrast that to other people who just give up when something doesn't go well or those of us who continue to make the same mistake over and over and over again because we fail to learn from our mistakes. These people never really grow and if they do, the growth is minimal. In order to grow you need to try new things and experience success and failure. If you keep from doing that, you will never become a one percenter.

One percenters also look at things and wonder how they could be better, faster or cheaper or just different. Instead of looking at how things are, they wonder how they could be! One percenters see opportunities where others see problems! They realize that whenever someone has a problem, they are looking for a solution. If you can provide that solution, you will be in demand and successful!

One percenters don't avoid the negative or look the other way; they look at it closely and see how they can turn those negatives into positives. Every product or service we have today is there because someone saw a need or a problem and created a solution for it! Instead of complaining about how something is, they instead spent their time figuring out how to make it better.

No matter what format you are reading this book in, you are reading it because someone saw a need for creating some way of bringing information to the people who need it.

If you are reading the paperback version you are reading it because Guttenberg built the printing press. If you are reading an electronic version it is because someone saw a need for people to carry a small device capable of holding many books. Your music player was born when someone decided carrying a bulky tape player that only held 30 songs wasn't the best solution!

You do not have to be an inventor in order to be a one percenter. But you need to change your way of looking at things so that you search out the positive instead of dwelling on the negative. You have to be able to look at today's issues with an eye for tomorrow!

The other thing the one percenter also does is to look ahead into the future and factor that in as well. Instead of doing what might be good for today, they look ahead and do what is also good for tomorrow as well. Sometimes doing something for long term gain or effect is much more valuable than doing what works just for today. One thing the one percenter certainly is not is short sighted!

It stands to reason that if we are to rise above most everyone else we have to think and act differently from them as well. We have to train ourselves to react properly and to take action when it needs to be taken. We need to become leaders and innovators and not be someone who stands in the shadows waiting for someone else to pave the way.

The question now is "How do I go about changing my attitude?" The answer is that we change things best when we understand the need for the change and then make changes slowly and gradually over time.

So start out by making a very conscious effort to find the good in everything negative. Train yourself to look for an opportunity even if you cannot take advantage of that opportunity. Get used to looking at everything from a positive point of view. Keep track of what you find by writing things down so you can refer back to them later.

Next, learn to embrace failure or acknowledge your mistakes. Look back at past failures, even though they might have been painful, and see what you did wrong or what you might have done differently. Look into them carefully and in detail. Learn from those mistakes so you will be better prepared for the next time you find yourself in the same or similar situation. This will make you stronger and stronger over time.

Next, force yourself to get out of your "comfort zone" and expose yourself to new and different things. Knowledge is power and one of the best ways to gain knowledge is to experience more things. Don't be afraid to learn from your mistakes, especially in the beginning. Everyone makes mistake while they are learning and you are no different. Learn, listen, observe and practice. Then evaluate your results and learn so more from them.

Last, but most certainly not least, demand and expect more from yourself. One of the largest roadblocks to success and being among the best is not giving yourself enough credit or expecting your best efforts.

One percenters expect to be at their best all of the time. This does not mean expecting to be perfect or demanding perfection from others but instead making the commitment to do their best at everything they try to do. Often this is the difference between success and failure or coming in second.

Life is a competition and we must learn to compete. We compete for opportunities, we compete at athletics and we compete for the attention and affection of others. Very little is handed to us in life and those that go out and work towards what they want will be the one who are successful.

The top in life are the ones who understand that their best efforts will get them the best results. If you are applying for a job you are competing against tens or hundreds of other people. You need to be at your best at every step of the process. If you let yourself take it easy, you may very well find yourself waiting for the next job while someone else gets the job.

While we are not suggesting that life is a winner take all process, it is a process where those who are willing to put in the time and effort are the ones who will reap the most benefits.

The most successful people realize this and embrace it. You do not necessarily have to like it or believe it, but you need to embrace it and work within it.

In order to get to be among the best you have to act like you are one of the best. That means developing the self confidence and attitude that successful people have. You must believe in yourself and your abilities. You cannot let failure defeat you. Instead it must make you stronger.

This is not some kind of magical process that requires magical powers and special education. It is an attitude and attitudes take time to develop. You need to make a commitment that starting today that you are going to move through life in a more confident manner. Take baby steps if you must but create a more confident you.

When people see you they should feel your confidence. They should feel that you are a person that needs to be taken seriously and respected for who and what you are. You should inspire other by what you do and what you have done. People should look up to you not because you demand that they do but instead because they want to.

Attitudes are wonderful things. We can create an attitude that makes us stronger and more successful. We can create attitudes that push us to go further than we ever thought possible. We can create attitudes that bring us success or we can create attitudes that help keep us down.

It's all within your grasp. Anyone can change their attitudes once they have the right motivation and the right approach. You can do this and you should do this!

Not it's up to you!

One Important Thing
for You to Decide

Do you have an ego? Some people do and it prevents them from seeing some things clearly and making the right decisions and judgments? If that sounds like you, then it is time that we come to terms with our ego and how it can either help or hinder our efforts to get to become a one percenter.

We all know people who find it more important to be right instead of happy. These are the people who will fight almost to the death before admitting they did something wrong or made any kind of mistake. These are also the people who often fail to take responsibility for their actions and seek to always find others to blame. You probably know a few of these people in your life. We all do because they are all around.

So we need you to make a decision right now before we go any further.

Are you going to allow your ego and personal pride to stand in the way of your success? Are you going to be one of those people who refuse to acknowledge a mistake or learn from it? Are you going to be one of those who stick to their position whether it's right or wrong?

Hopefully you are going to decide to be someone who will not let their personal feelings or agenda to interfere with doing what is right. Hopefully you will keep an open mind when you are challenged and be able to see things for what they really are instead of what you need them to be. Hopefully you will be able to deal with the reality of life instead of how you want things to be.

One percenters have personal confidence and conviction in all that they do but they still keep themselves grounded in reality. If they are involved in something that is not working right, they will be open-minded to look at something objectively and deal with it. They will not continue to do what doesn't work just because they designed it that way. They will listen to others and accept criticism gracefully.

For example, if a successful person created a product that didn't sell well, they would make sure the design and appearance as well as the marketing and everything else was good.

If all of that was deemed good and the product still didn't sell, they would chalk it up to experience and move on. Someone who was more concerned with their ego might continue to dedicated money and other resources into something that likely will never be successful. They would do all this because this was their project and something they designed. In other words, they would turn a blind eye to reality.

Can you place your ego to the side and do what's right? Can you separate pride from reality and move above it? Can you force yourself to stand back and look at things objectively?

If you can do that then there is great hope for you. Being able to do that successfully and consistently will enable you to move ahead of many other people who do not possess those abilities. It will lead you down the path to success and cause you to become more productive. It will also allow you to cut your losses and get more out of life as well.

So what's it going to be? Which path are you going to head down?

What Do You REALLY Want?

It seems that everyone wants to be successful in life but it would amaze you how many people never really give much thought as to what success really means to them. Without knowing what you are looking for in life, how will you ever begin to go about finding it? More important, if you are not aware of what you really want, would you even realize it when you find it?

What if what you really wanted and treasured was the time you had to spend with your family but you took a job that kept you away from home for weeks or months at a time? Would you be happy with that? Would you consider that success? Would you really have the drive to become a one percenter for something you didn't like and didn't want?

Probably not.

One thing one percenters know is what is important to them and what they value in life. Those things cannot be copied from someone else. There is no one perfect approach for life just as there is not one universal set of morals and values. We are all different and one of those differences is how we see our lives and how we live them.

It is important to your long term success and productivity that whatever you choose to do in life that it be something that means something to you. It should be more than money, fame or power. It should be something that resonates within you deep down in your soul. It should be something that gives you a sense of fulfillment, accomplishment, satisfaction and appreciation. It should be something that makes you smile at the end of each day.

It has been said that if someone does something they really love and enjoy that they will never really work a single day in their life. That is because when we do the things we love, we enjoy ourselves. We are more willing to put in the extra time and effort that is often needed to do a great job.

One percenters understand this and do more of what they like and enjoy in life. They are able to do that because they took the time to look deep down within themselves to discover what it is that they really wanted out of life.

Maybe it was money or power but often those are just things we think we want but really don't even break the top 10 on our list of important things.

So how do you go about determining what you really want out of your life? Well, you start by taking the time to look inside yourself to find out what brings you satisfaction and a sense of fulfillment? Ask yourself what makes you feel good and what makes you feel sad? What makes you smile? What makes you happy?

Write all of these things down and then head over to the opposite side. What makes you feel sad? What makes you feel angry? What things mean absolutely nothing to you? Write those things down as well.

Sometimes it's hard to come with everything. Some things may disguise themselves a bit by hiding inside other things. So ask yourself what were the happiest times in your life? When you were your happiest and what were you doing at that particular time. Break it down and dissect it until you get down to the basics.

Sometimes the process is pretty straight forward and other times it will take you on a roller coaster ride through the ups and downs of life. But if you stick with it, you will soon emerge with a pretty good understanding of what really means something to you and what you treasure in life.

When you look at things, patterns usually appear that you were not aware of. Common threads run through all your experiences and that one common thread gives you the main part of your life that has real meaning for you.

For example, let's say you wrote down the five happiest times in your life and included in those times were the day you met your spouse, a family vacation, the birth of your son or daughter and the quiet nights around the campfire you spent as a child during your summer family vacation.

The one common thread in all of those experiences was that you were with family and people who loved you. Money was never a part of those experiences, at least in your memory it wasn't. Neither was power or fame or anything like that. You were the happiest when you were alone with family and quietly enjoying life.

Now you might have changed since then and you probably have. The same things we loved as children we probably have outgrown by now. But the underlying attraction and appeal is still there. That is what we need to reveal and get out in the open.

If your happiest memories consisted of starting your company, landing your first big deal, and watching your company grow, then that would mean you were a different person than the fellow who loved to spend time with family.

For you it is all about career and personal accomplishments. You enjoy the power, the money and the prestige that comes along with building your own business. That's who you are and that's what you need to be as long as you still feel that way.

Now if you put the family man in a position where he had to work 80 hours a week, the high salary, power and prestige would mean very little because he would miss his family time. If you took the businessman and gave him a 40 hour a week job and made him spend nights and weekends with his family he would not be happy either. Neither view is right or wrong. It all depends on the person and their values, morals, likes and dislikes.

You cannot look at your successful friend and say "I want to be just like him" because what you like might be totally incompatible with what he likes. His lifestyle, though perfect for him might be horrible for you. There is no one perfect approach to life and because we are all different there is no one perfect action plan, either.

The one percenter understands the value of understanding who we are and what makes us "tick". They understand the need to know what makes us what we are and what we need to do to achieve what we value in life. In other words, the one percenter knows the value of knowing which is the right direction to move in order to get what we really want.

Don't be someone who thinks they know what they want. Be the person who KNOWS what they really want. Be the person who knows which direction they need to go in and what their real goals and ambitions should be.

Don't be someone who wastes time and resources pursuing someone else's dreams. Be the person who takes control over their own lives and goes after what they want and not what someone else feels is best for them.

One Percenters understand that they need to understand themselves before they can understand anything else. They understand the need to understand their past so they can plan their future. This isn't hard and it doesn't require any special skills or knowledge.

It requires just one small thing. All of us have it but some of us don't use it. The "thing" I am referring to is............

The Need to be Honest

We have been talking a lot about introspection, attitudes and understanding our past. We have talked about understanding who we are and what we need to do moving forward. All of this is important because we need to make every effort to choose the right path and move in the right direction. In other words, if we are going to become the best and do our best, we have to be doing the right things in life.

But we also need to understand one more thing. We need to understand why it is so vitally important that we always be honest with ourselves and others. It is important to be honest with ourselves because sometimes the decisions we make in life will be made according to information we tell ourselves is true. If that information is false, then we stand a good chance of making the wrong decisions.

Telling the truth is sometimes hard. It sometimes can cause us embarrassment or cause hard feelings. Lying sometimes appears easier but lying usually comes back to catch up with us later and make things worse. But even worse than lying to others is lying to ourselves. Some of us do that on a regular basis. And we need to do something about that and we need to do it right this minute.

If we lie to ourselves then we are hurting ourselves. Telling ourselves that we want something different than the truth is never a good idea. It can send us off in the wrong direction and cost us lost time and resources. While we may go ahead and achieve our goals, those goals will likely be the wrong goals and we will have to start all over. All because we were afraid to admit the truth about ourselves.

One percenters know they need to be 100% honest with themselves no matter how painful or eye opening the experience might be. They understand that experiencing a little bit of pain now will help us much more later. They also understand why they should never let their pride or ego overcome being honest.

If you ask yourself a question, then you owe it to yourself to give yourself an honest answer. If you don't know the answer you look for the truth and accept the truth. You do not convince yourself of something that is not the truth just because it is what you want to hear.

If you have to make a decision, base that decision on the truth and facts and not on what you wish things were like. Make informed decisions that will move you toward your goals and not base those decisions on fantasy and lies. You have only yourself to blame when you lie. You cannot move forward in the right direction when you base everything on lies and deceit.

Now is the time to ask yourself how honest you have been with yourself up to this point. Have you been truthful in your judgments and analysis? Have you been accurate and truthful when it comes to your abilities and performance? Or have you made yourself out to be someone you're not? Have you been truthful about who and what you are so far in life?

We can change those things that we acknowledge. We can become better and more honest people if we truly want to. All we need to do is stop being dishonest and start telling ourselves the truth.

Keep in mind that the exercises and tasks in this book can be done and kept strictly between you and your own mind. You do not have to share your thoughts and your answers with anyone if you don't want to. Once you understand that, you see there is no reason to lie to yourself. The only one who hears the answers to some difficult questions is you.

And that is the best person to hear those answers!

Accept Responsibility

One percenters believe that what they do they should either take credit for or accept the responsibility for. They understand the importance of standing behinds what you do and how you do it. There are many ways to get things done and some of them are more honest and effective than others. If you truly want to get to the top of your craft or profession, you need to learn how to accept responsibility.

We all make mistakes and we all have errors in judgment. People expect that of each other and usually understand unless they feel the error or deed was done on purpose. But what we do after we take action is often more important than the action itself. Do we run and hide or do we stand up and take responsibility for our action? Do we look for others to blame or work behind the scenes to deflect blame to others? How we react says a lot about our personal integrity and values.

We all know people who hide from accepting blame or taking responsibility for the things they do in life. We also know how we feel about these people and those thoughts are usually not very positive. Personal integrity is a very important factor in how successful people become in their area of expertise. No one wants to be associated with someone who looks to deflect blame or shirk from their responsibilities.

People with that attitude are usually not thought highly of when it comes time for promotion or awards. They are viewed as negatives when compared to other people. Opportunities are not plentiful for those people either. In order to take advantage of an opportunity these people have to hope the opportunity comes from people who don't know them. Even then they have to hope that no one who is contacted regarding your application makes the company aware of the type of person they really are.

But let's for a moment say that you don't care about any of that. Your moral compass is just fine with you blaming others and walking away scot free. Your values tell you that anything you do that turns out good is worth it no matter how much you blame or hurt someone else. We all know people like that and let's assume you are one of them.

There is still one important benefit in accepting responsibility and you really should be aware of it.

Not because it's the right thing to do (and it is!) but because it will help you grow and increase your knowledge at the same time! Do I have your attention now? I certainly hope so!

Our brains work on what we feel and experience in our lives. Everything we do results in something that we experience. If we do something that works out well, we will do the same, or close to the same, thing next time. If we read something we feel is important or relevant, we will remember it for longer periods of time than something we feel we will never use.

The stronger the impact on our minds, the more we experience and the more we learn. That helps us grow faster and learn more than we would ever have learned from a book or lecture. Sometimes even the worst experience turns out to be a blessing in disguise because we picked up a ton of knowledge from the experience. Knowledge that will be solidly stored in our minds for next time and the time after that.

But a funny thing happens when we don't take responsibility for what we do and how we do it. When we deflect blame or run away, we never fully experience the effects of what we had done. So we never get to really learn everything we could have had we stepped up and taken responsibility.

Little details or feedback we might have received might go to someone else and that information, that could have been used to keep us from making the same mistakes in the future, will never be processed!

As we said, everyone makes mistakes. It is not so much the mistakes we make as what we do with them after we make them. One percenters, and other successful people, learn from their mistakes and this helps them become better, smarter and more prepared for what comes next. If you make a mistake and never learn from it, you will continue to make those same mistakes over and over and over again. You will continue to waste time and resources and fail to make any progress in life.

One percenters understand the more you learn and the faster you grow, the earlier you will find yourself prepared for opportunities as they come along. They understand that taking the easier approach now often hurts you later. So they do the right thing now to help them become more prepared for what comes next.

They also understand that how they do things has a direct impact on everyone around them. They also understand why they need to do things the right way and stand up for whatever might arise from those actions. You cannot form good relationships with people you work with or interact with if you do not hold yourself accountable for what you do.

You will lose the trust of the people who might be people who can help you get to the next level in your career.

You might offend someone who will pass over your name when they are asked if they know someone they could recommend for a great new job at another company. In some cases, you might anger the wrong people and they might plot against you to get back at you for what you have done to them. Regardless of the outcome, this is something you need to address very quickly.

I try and stay away from morals and values because they vary widely among different people. But no matter what your values and morals might be, taking responsibility for the things you do in life should always be in your values and moral code. Not because it is a lofty goal or value and not because you want to take the moral high ground.

It should be in your values because it is a very basic and critical value for everyone. It should never be OK to blame someone else for something you did. It should never be OK to make someone else suffer because of your actions. And it should never be OK for you to benefit by making others take the fall for your mistakes.

Some people actually believe that doing that kind of thing can make you rise to the top very quickly. In some cases they might even be right.

But when people get to the top by stepping on people in the process, their fall from the top is swift and usually devastating. That is because they leave a trail of angry people below them who will never lift a finger again to help or support them when needed.

The one great thing is that it is easy to start taking responsibility in your life. It requires nothing more than an attitude change. All you need to do is be aware of what you are doing now and realize what things you need to change. It sounds simple and it can be if you are willing to be honest with yourself.

First, if you always look to blame others when things don't go the way they should have gone, look at yourself first to see if you might have done something differently or better. If you discover something you did that was even partially responsible for, take responsibility for it. Look in you first and only after you do that look at others.

Second, if you make excuses or try to rationalize something you did, stop that as well. There may be reasons why you did what you did but if those reasons were wrong, you still made a mistake. Instead, understand why those reasons were wrong and learn how to move on and do better next time. As we said, learn from your mistakes don't perpetuate them!

Third, never try and make yourself look better by making everyone else look worse. This should not even have to be discussed but some people really do this in life and you shouldn't be one of them. Always work on making yourself, and those around you, better. You will not only gather the respect and admiration of others in the process, you will get stronger as well.

Fourth, just be honest with yourself and others. Make the best decisions possible using as much information and data as you can and then be right there front and center regardless of how things turn out. Don't hide in the background and wait for others to realize it was your fault. Stand up and acknowledge it and move on.

Once percenters understand the need to create a positive impression in the minds of others. They understand that by accepting responsibility for what they do and how they do it they will actually go further in life in less time than many other people.

That is because in the process of taking or accepting responsibility they have created something very strong and powerful. Something that will help them every single day as they go through life. Something that will open doors and create more opportunities for them. Do you know what that one thing is?

Well, we'll get to that next.......

Your Reputation

Let's spend a moment discussing one more thing that will get damaged by your failure or unwillingness to accept responsibility. That one thing that will become quickly damaged is your reputation. Even if you don't give a you know what about what people think of you, it's still important when it comes to advancing in life.

Your reputation is perhaps the single most important thing you have going for you. Or, it can be the biggest obstacle you may have to overcome if that reputation is very bad. Your reputation is important because it not only follows you wherever you go, it sometimes precedes you and helps either pave the way for you or slams the door in your face!

It is also important to understand that your reputation is a **perception** in the minds of other people.

It is how they perceive you to be. This can be very accurate or inaccurate depending on how that perception was created. While this is not fair, it is the way these things go in life. People think a certain way and they develop perceptions based on how they perceive something to be.

So not only do you have to worry about factual things when it comes to your reputation, you will have to concern yourself with other factors as well. That means how others feel about you, what they say about you, and how the things you do are interpreted by others. All of these things, plus possibly a few more, are thrown together and your reputation emerges. It is up to you to do the things, and create the proper atmosphere around you, necessary to create a very positive reputation.

One percenters understand just how important your reputation is when it comes to getting more of what they want in life. They understand that a good reputation will make you worth more to others and make yourself more desirable in the marketplace and in life. This translates into more people feeling highly about you and more willing to either recommend you to others or to promote you from within.

One percenters understand that life and success are competitions and when you are in any kind of competition you should do everything in your power to gain a legitimate edge over everyone else.

When it comes to taking advantage of an opportunity, you need to be the one who sticks out above the rest. You need to have the best background, the best education and impress others that you are the best overall candidate for the job.

One percenters understand the value and role your reputation plays in this entire process. You want to be known as someone who can be counted upon when needed. You want to be known as someone who is always trustworthy and honest. Most of all, you want to be known as a person of integrity. When you are known for all of these things and more, people will be drawn to you and want to interact with you.

If you truly want to become a one percenter, you have to be willing to put yourself "out there" in your town, your industry and wherever people in your same area of expertise are noticed or seen. You need to get out and get noticed. But even more important than where you should go, you should be asking yourself "What will people "see" when they hear about me?"

We already mentioned that your reputation can actually precede you in life. That means that people may often hear about you even before they meet you. Your reputation will let them know in advance what kind of person you are and whether or not they should want to be associated with you.

So based on what they hear, you will either have the road to success already paved for you or you will have a mountain to climb just to get back to square one!

So now that we agree that our reputation is critical to our success, the question we should now be asking is "How can I create the very best reputation possible?" Note I said "the very best reputation" and not "a good reputation." That is because we need to remember we are in a competition and "good enough" is usually not good enough. We want to be at our best, not half best!

We build our reputation over time. One cannot create a reputation in a day or a week or even a month. Sometimes it takes year or several years to develop the right reputation. You develop it by creating a history of good experiences with other people. If you are new to an area or a company it might be faster and easier to create that perfect reputation because you will have no past data to overcome. But regardless of whether you are somewhere for 14 years or 14 minutes, you have to establish a pattern of good behavior and positive experiences.

I say that you need to establish a pattern of experiences because one or two experiences are not enough to create a new perception. You need many experiences and they all need to be positive in nature. Anything negative will set you and your reputation back. Negative experiences also carry more "weight" than positive experiences as well.

If you "mess up" and create a negative experience, it might take as many as 10 positive experiences to counter the effect of that one negative experience. Because of this, we must always be on guard to do our very best when it comes to doing anything in life. Again, good enough will usually not be good enough. This is important because sometimes you just won't have the opportunity to get those 10 more chances to erase the negative one!

So what are some positive things we can do to improve our reputation? What are the things other people and employers look for in others? While the list might be different for any particular position or situation, here are a few of the most important and critical overall factors you should consider when crafting your reputation:

Honesty

We should always be completely honest in everything we do. That means never lying or doing anything that could even be possibly considered dishonest. This is one of those issues that are really driven by perception. If you are caught doing something even slightly questionable, some people will draw their own conclusions and believe if you would to that you would be capable of doing much worse.

Integrity

Integrity means being true to who you are and what you believe in. It means holding true to your values and morals and not being willing to sacrifice anything to get what you want. This is something that is greatly admired by other in society today. That is because it appears that fewer and fewer people place much value in their own personal integrity. Always remember that your integrity can also take years to build and just seconds or minutes to destroy!

Ethical

Ethical people do things right. Not just right procedure-wise but within established ethical and moral values. They do not cheat others in order to get ahead and they don't throw laws, rules and regulations aside to achieve their own goals.

People with high ethics are in high demand because of the extreme exposure and liability that a company might get if someone were to try anything illegal or against any rules or regulations. The other factor is that the reputation of the company is at stake whenever someone does anything in the name of the company.

As far as individuals are concerned, ethics are important because people want to do business with outer ethical people so as to not find themselves associating with people who may damage their own reputation.

Reliability

People like other people who do what they said they were going to do and who are there when they said they will be. They want to be able to trust and believe that someone will respond like they stated they would and in an appropriate time frame as well. Very little in this world is done by just one person and in order for any project to remain on schedule everyone must do what they are supposed to do and they must also do that within the stated time frames.

Willingness to Work

The world is full of people who talk a good game but then are not willing to put in the time and effort required to do the job right. Companies and other people want someone who is willing to do what is needed to get the job done. That means being willing to roll up your sleeves and get it done even though it might not be your responsibility to do so.

That might mean arriving early and leaving late when extra time is required to get something done on schedule. It means taking responsibility for certain tasks even though they are assigned to someone else in order to get the job done.

In other words, they are not looking for the person who says "It's not my job." and moves on. They want someone committed to getting things done no matter what it takes.

Positive Attitude

People with a positive attitude are more productive and get more done in less time than those people who just stand around and complain about things. Companies and associates look for people who concentrate on what is right rather than obsessing on what's wrong.

People with positive attitudes are also more adept at working through problems because they see past the negatives and see what is working right. Then they look for the flaw and correct it. Negative people just see the negative and look no further. Even if the resolution is simple they just don't bother to look for it.

Enthusiastic

Enthusiastic people are hard to come by these days. When someone loves what they do and is enthusiastic throughout the process that attitude quickly becomes contagious. This further increases both productivity and the quality of the results. This is an extension of the positive attitude. Someone who is enthusiastic takes pride in their work and is thrilled by being able to make something positive happen.

Articulate

The best ideas might not seem that great if you can't articulate them well.

You will never be able to get your point across if your communication skills are not where they should be.

People who know how to speak intelligently are also appreciated and in great demand because they impress other people and help create the impression that the person knows what they are talking about. This inspires confidence and trust in that person and who they represent.

People who cannot communicate or converse well are perceived to be less qualified and less knowledgeable than others even if that is not necessarily the case. In order to become known as the best in your profession you need to make people feel you are the best. The best way to start doing that is learning how to speak and converse on a high level.

Persistent

Many times success is just a step away but people get discouraged and quit. People who know what they want or what needs to be done and do not give up until they achieve their objective are in high demand. You want to be known as the person who keeps at it until they reach their objectives. Just doing this will place you above most other people in this world today.

Self-Confident

We discussed perception and this is one area where perception really matters. In order to get to the top today you need to be confident in your skills and abilities. You need to know what you can do and not be afraid to go ahead and do it. You must be able to make others feel this way as well.

Confident people give others the impression that they are highly skilled and very proficient at what they do. They create the perception that there is no one better or more qualified for any particular task or situation. They believe that you are the "go to" person and that you are the most qualified.

On the flip side, people who are meek and unsure of themselves appear weaker and less qualified than others. These are the people who are rarely chosen not because they aren't qualified but rather because they give the impression that they are weaker than others.

Self-Disciplined

The higher up the ladder you move the more you will be required and expected to work with little to no supervision. While you may be held accountable to someone else, the day to day tasks and responsibilities will be left up to you.

You must develop a reputation for being able to work on your own without constant supervision. You must create the impression that you can take a task through to completion without missing a deadline or being reminded that something is due on a certain date.

People like people who know what needs to be done once they are told and that's it. No constant reminders, no missing deadlines and very little hand holding throughout the process.

There are many other traits that can help you create a perfect impression but most of those are very similar to the ones we just listed. If you can work on the items in this chapter, that will bring you a long way towards your goals and objectives.

Just remember that building your reputation is a constant process and you are never really done. You are always being judged and evaluated on what you most recently done. One percenters agreed that while you can lean on your reputation to help you succeed, you must always build on that relationship by always doing things well and right today.

They also agree that even the best reputation can suffer a setback or two along the way.

But if you constantly strive to do your best and always do what's right, many things just take care of themselves in the process. So do what's right, always play by the rules, never just do the minimum and never look for the easy way out.

Those are the building blocks of a great reputation.

Putting Life in Drive

By now you have hopefully decided that you really want to be among the very best and you are willing to make the necessary changes to do so. If that is where you are then I salute you because you have already taken one of the most important and significant steps you need to achieve that goal. You have taken the step that many people refuse to take. You have taken the first step and for many, that is the very hardest.

So for taking that first step, you should be congratulated. You are not one of those who let their egos and their need to always be right interfere with you getting the happiness in life that you deserve.

Now it's time to take the second step and the second step is just as easy and just as powerful.

The second step is making a commitment to yourself to always look at things before you do them and make sure that they meet one specific criteria. This is something almost every one percenter does every day of their lives.

So what is this magic criteria?

Moving forward, from this day on, you must always ask yourself one very important question before you decide on anything or do anything. That question is "Will this bring me closer to my goals or move me further away from them?" If you ask this one question, most things will become much clearer and you will be able to make better and more accurate decisions and judgments.

Stop and think about that for a minute. What you are doing is making sure that what you are about to do is really the right thing for you at that point in time. You are thinking about what the repercussions of something are going to mean down the road for you in life. Just by stopping to think about something gives you the ability to look at it from another point of view. Often that is enough to stop us from doing something that might not be the smartest thing for us to do.

For example, let's say you are considering whether you should study for an important test or go to the movies with your friends. Now you really want to see that movie and you like going out with your friends so the attraction can be very strong.

But if you ask yourself the "magic question" you will think about it another way.

You will think about how getting a better grade might help you get into a better school or open a few more doors for you in the future. So studying for that test becomes something that you not only should do, but it also makes sense to you as far as your future is concerned. You can always see that movie tomorrow night instead of tonight.

You can ask yourself that question when it comes time to decide which type of education you want to go after or what is best for your career. On a smaller level, you might be tempted to not put in your best effort on something because you really don't have the time at that moment. We all find ourselves in that type of situation and sometimes we don't do what we really should. The magic question will help you with that.

One major difference between the one percenter and everyone else is that they try to move through life by always doing things that advance them towards their goals and stay away from those things that take them further away from them. Are they always successful? No, they're not. But they do the right things most of the time to get them closer to their goals.

Most major successes in life are not the result of one huge act or event. They are the result of many things that happened in the past that lead up to the overall success.

These are the little things we do every day that help us prepare for events and opportunities are usually the most important factors when it comes to being a success.

While this is good because little things are usually easier and faster to accomplish, one potential danger is that we often do not place much importance the little things even though they may pay huge dividends for us later on. So we give those things little effort and often do not do as good a job as we could have.

Think of think of the times in your past when you could have done something better, or produced a better result and you didn't because you just felt it really didn't matter. This is not a personality defect because we all feel that way at some points in our lives. But the difference between a one percenter and everyone else is that they are far more discerning about when they let that happen.

One percenters approach life by thinking things through and doing only those things that bring them closer to their goals and aspirations. If something makes sense for now and the future, they will do it. If it doesn't, they will pass on doing that and do something that makes better sense to them. Often these decisions might seem minor, even inconsequential in nature, but they help them get what they want faster than it might take other people.

One perfect example of this is procrastination. While some people might put something off until tomorrow because they don't need it right this minute, the one percenter is going to look at it and ask, "Is it better to do this now or put it off until later? Which will get me closer to my goals? Which will prepare me better for what lies ahead?" The answer to those questions will direct them on the right way to proceed.

For example, let's say the next stage of one's career or goals are to get certified in financial management or any other profession. This will entail taking some classes, getting some experience and probably taking an examination or two. None of those things are particularly pleasant or easy to do and the temptation might be to put it off for a while.

But the one percenter will ask the questions and come up with the answers. They will understand that they are better off getting the certification now so they will be able to take advantage of any opportunity that might come along sooner rather than later. That would be perceived as a benefit.

For example, while they might plan on getting that new job in two years when the person currently holding it retires, that opportunity might come earlier, or the same opportunity at another company might become available and only those people who are ready with that certification in hand will qualify!

They will also see the benefit in doing something now when they know they will have the time rather than waiting until later when time might be unavailable. Life is unpredictable and no one knows what is going to come up next and possibly make it difficult to do something when needed.

For example, you have a report due in a month and you could easily do it today but you decide to take a two hour lunch instead and relax. After all, you have worked hard this week. But three weeks later, a big deal comes up requiring all your time to draft a new proposal and business plan. Not only will you have to do that work, but you will still have that report that needs to be done and now you don't have the time to do it without working late nights.

If I were to put this all into one summary, I would tell you that life is a series of events and opportunities. While most people prefer to take their lives one day at a time and proceed through life at a leisurely pace, the one percenters understand that those people who are prepared and ready for opportunities when they come around are the ones who have the most chance of success.

They understand that it is beneficial to move through life at your own pace making sure things get done and actions are taken on their schedule rather than being forced into working under tight deadlines.

They understand that living in that manner is less stressful and almost always allows them to dedicate more time and effort and create higher quality results.

The one percenters understand that life is one big competition and in order to compete effectively you always have to be at your best and do your best. They understand that it is in their benefit to do the things they need to do before they really need to do them.

They live their lives constantly doing things to move them further ahead. They constantly take action that makes them better, more prepared and more valuable to others. They don't do this some of the time; they do it ALL the time. Yes, they also relax and they also have fun. But they understand there is a time and place for relaxation and fun and a time and place for doing what needs to be done.

So now you have a choice. You can go through life living from day to day doing what needs to be done for right now and let the future take care of itself. That might work for you but it leaves a lot to chance.

Or you can start doing the things you can do now to help you now and prepare you for later. You can look into the future and do right now to prepare yourself for what lies ahead. You don't wait until you need something in order to do it. You understand the need and you take care of it now rather than later.

The wonderful part about adapting this kind of constantly moving forward attitude is that once you start it, life becomes much easier and a lot less stressful. You can move forward in your life and not get caught unaware or unprepared. You will most always be ready and able to take care of every opportunity that might come your way. Even when you are caught unaware you will almost always have less to catch up on than others who often wait until the last minute.

You will find that only doing the things that help bring you closer to what you want in life will also save you countless hours of wasted time and a ton of wasted resources! That means getting more done in less time and making more progress in your life as well. While other people are recovering from their mistakes, you are moving forward and rarely looking back!

This is one of those situations where taking the easier road to something is really the best thing for you to do. It makes much more sense to work smarter than harder when you have the chance.

I want you to learn how to make the right moves, the right decisions and always move forward. Take baby steps if you must but take those steps at every opportunity. Make it your goal to make at least one move forward every single day. Whether that is something major or something small, just make that move and take that step.

Remember that all these little steps add up to major advances over time. It is better to make steady progress at a slower rate than to try and do too much at one time and get overwhelmed and discouraged.

Adopt the attitude all one percenters have. Go through each and every day moving forward closer to your goals, dreams and aspirations. Make only the moves that bring you closer and stay away from things that take you further away.

This will lead you closer to success and happiness than you ever thought possible.

Do What Others Refuse to Do!!

Here is a quick and easy way to get ahead in this world and achieve success. Your road to becoming a one percenter will go much faster if you just grasp this one simple attitude adjustment.

Just be willing to check your ego at the door and do the things that many other people just refuse to do. Just be willing to do something you think is "beneath you" because it will help you get closer to what you want to achieve. It's a simple yet very effective way at looking at things that seems to escape most people.

One percenters understand that if something needs to get done to bring them to the next step in their plan, then THEY are responsible for making sure that happens. It makes no difference whether it is our responsibility or not.

If YOU need something to happen or get done, then YOU are responsible for making sure that it happens. Even if YOU have to do it yourself!

One percenters ask themselves who stands to benefit by something getting done. If the answer is that they will benefit, then they make sure whatever needs to get done gets done. It's not rocket science!

For example, if you want to sell your house and someone is coming to look at it, you want it to look its very best. That's because the better it looks, the higher the price someone will be willing to pay for it. After all, if someone drives up and the place looks gorgeous, they will be more impressed. If it looks messy or ugly, they might still buy it but they will offer less money.

So let's say you are showing the house to someone at 2 o'clock. You get to the house in the morning and see the landscaper never came and the lawn is too high and uneven. Some people might say "Oh, the heck with it. I'm not mowing any lawn. That's not my job." Then they go ahead and sell the house for $200,000.

The one percenter would say "Oh, well, I'll mow it, make it look nice and make more money." They spend two hours mowing and trimming the lawn and make the house look great. They buyer loves it and buys it for $220,000 because it was the best house they saw and his wife loved it.

Now if someone told you they would give you $20,000 to mow their lawn, would you say "That's not my job?" Of course not! You would mow 10 lawns for $20K a pop! The funny thing is, this is not an exaggeration! The "curb appeal" of any house is critical to people coming to look at your house! It can make or break a sale and bring in tens of thousands more in profits!

Once percenters understand the real value in doing some tasks themselves. They do not tell themselves they are too good to do menial labor and they don't let their egos get in the way either. If they see a valid reason to do something, they just go ahead and do it. They don't worry about what others think or how it might look to be seen doing those tasks.

Life is full of things we don't like or want to do. The difference between being a one percenter and everyone else is that if we see the value in doing something, we go ahead and do it. Whatever it might be, if it makes sense to do it we will do it. If we see the benefit, we will do it. If it has to get done and no one else will do it, we will do it.

You make think this sounds foolish and perhaps it does. But there are people today who refuse to take a lower paying job to feed their families because they feel that those jobs are beneath them. We have people who refuse to do a job because it is messy or smelly or for who knows what reason. But the one percenter looks at these things differently.

Entire businesses and careers have been created just from doing things other people don't like to do. There are people making more than doctors or engineers or other professionals and they are getting top dollar to do jobs like cleaning up pet waste or cleaning gutters! These are not difficult tasks but there are certain people who would gladly pay someone else to do it for them.

I'm not saying you have to make a career out of doing things you don't want to do. Quite the contrary, I'm telling you that sometimes you will NEED to do certain things in order to move ahead to the next level. When those times arrive, do not be the one who refuses out or ego or vanity. Instead, be the one who sees a need, understands the reason and just goes out and does it.

It's a simple thing that can really make a huge difference. If you doubt this even for one minute, go to the library and take out a few biographies on some really successful people. You will see that most, if not all, of them got down and dirty I their early days doing what it took to building their business or create their fortune.

One percenters gladly do those things now so they won't have to do them later. It is absolutely amazing how many people fail to grasp this simple concept and hold themselves back just because they refused to do something other people would.

Set Higher Standards

Life is full of measurements, evaluations, comparisons and standards. These are the things we find ourselves measured against, compared with and judged by. Though there needs to be some way to measure someone's abilities or performance, sometimes these standards or comparisons get in the way of achievement.

One basic difference between most people and the one percenters or the people that want to achieve more out of life, is that most of the time they hold themselves to a higher standard than others do. Simply put, what might be acceptable to others is not acceptable to them.

This is a very important distinction because if you hold yourself to a higher standard than others expect of you, it will be rare that you fail to impress someone or deliver something that is not acceptable to your customer or boss.

That means you make people happy more often and at the same time create a reputation for exceeding expectations on a regular basis.

This does not mean that the one percenter creates unreasonable demands from his or herself or from people who do work for them or with them. Instead, they hold themselves accountable for what they honestly believe can be reached or achieved in that particular situation.

For example, let's say that you are a salesperson and your boss assigns you a goal of selling $1,000,000 worth of product in your territory this year. You look at your territory and honestly feel that your market could easily sustain $1,250,000 in sales so you take that into consideration and set your personal expectations at $1,200,000.

Now if you hit your personal goal, you automatically hit your assigned goal. In fact, you exceed the goal which means your boss is happy and you are looked at as having done an excellent job. You have exceeded their expectations by achieving your expectations!

If you always reach for more than what is expected you achieve several things at the same time. You deliver more to others than expected and that is always a good thing. You show yourself as someone who gets the job done and at the same time you prove to yourself what you can achieve when you put your mind to it.

This means that yearly evaluations are a breeze because you accomplished more than required. That leads to higher salary raises and bonuses in the future.

This means that you will gain more business because you delivered more to your customer than you originally promised. This will help your business or company grow faster as word gets around throughout the industry.

This means that your supervisor will see you as being more productive and higher performing than most everyone else. That will lead to more opportunities and advancement in the future.

But there is also something else working in the background that actually makes it easier to do more than it is to do less! When you hold yourself to a higher standard, you alter how you go about achieving things at the same time. That's because you set your goals higher and create plans and solutions according to those higher goals.

Let's take the sales goal example and discuss that. You were assigned a goal of $1,000,000 but you set your personal goal at $1,200,000. So as you develop plans and processes designed to bring in $1,200,000 this year, you get yourself started at a faster level. So you have created a "buffer zone" in case the market slows or something else happens. If you bring in $100,000 a month you will hit your personal goal.

You will achieve that because of more focused and aggressive sales practices. Everyone else is bringing in $83,000 to hit their $1,000,000 goal and if something goes wrong or if the market slows they are behind!

But if things go wrong or if the market gets slower, you will have higher sales up front while the others don't. Your more aggressive goals set early on will help you compensate for unforeseen downturns! So your higher expectations set upfront will help you remain on tack while others fall behind.

One percenters understand it is always better to deal with things from a position of strength. If you exceed your goal while every else makes theirs, that is good. But if you achieve your goal when everyone else doesn't, the spotlight is on you because you were the only one who hit their goal! This sets you apart from everyone else and it gives you the recognition and visibility you need to succeed!

The other reason to set your personal goals or aspirations higher is that it is always good to impress people by doing a better job than what they expected or wanted. These days some people expect a certain level and you won't make much of an impression if you hit that level. In that case you did what was expected and that's it.

People don't get noticed for doing what they are supposed to do. They get recognized for doing more than what was expected or for doing less. No one gets a pat on the back for performing like everyone else.

But when we demand more of ourselves and hold ourselves accountable to us first and then others, we can improve the quality of our work, increase our productivity and make ourselves more valuable at the same time. That is because our attitude towards what we do and who we are has changed.

Contrast that to the person who thinks that as long as he or she does only what is asked or expected that everything would be just fine. They do not do anything more than what they are told and perform no better than whatever goals are set. In other words, if the goals are low, we will perform to that level. If the goals are too high, we will view them as unrealistic.

Our goal should not be to stay in the middle of the pack. People do not get to be successful or near the top of their profession by staying in the middle of the pack or performing like everyone else. People who do that are the people who routinely become the victims of budget cuts and downsizing.

One percenters understand you don't get to be in the top one percent by performing at a 50% level. They understand that in order to be the best you have to act like the best.

And in order to act like the best you have to perform like the best. That means holding yourself to a higher level.

Now if you agree with me on this, and there is no valid reason why you would not agree, then let's get started changing the way we look at things and how we are going to act moving forward.

The next time you are given a task along with some guidelines or expectations, take some time to figure out how reasonable those expectations really are. If they appear a little low, then create your own personal goals that are a bit more aggressive. You don't have to share them with anyone as they are your own private goals. But try and figure out ways to just not do what is asked, but do a little bit more. This will help you plan more effectively and get your thought process set on something higher and better.

Do this any time you are assigned a goal or a certain level of expectation. Write down your assigned goal and your personal goal. Maybe make a commitment to beat every assigned goal by 5% or 10%. It doesn't really make a difference on the amount of the increase. What's important is that you expect more of yourself than others do.

Then track your performance and your efforts. Always look for ways to make things better or ways to improve.

Never allow anyone else to tell you when you are good enough. Because good enough is usually not good enough to get to become a one percenter.

Setting Goals

I'm going to start off by saying that I hate goals. But even after saying that I am also going to say that goals most definitely have their place in allowing people to achieve their best in life. Goals allow us the ability to define where we are and where we want to go. Even more important, goals allow us to identify tasks and objectives we need to complete and give us a means to measure our progress.

The problem with goals is that we either have too many of them or that they are not realistic. Some of the time we have goals that are counter-productive. That means doing something to achieve one goal makes it more difficult to achieve another goal. This can be very frustrating.

But for the purpose of this book, we are going to discuss goals that we set for ourselves and how to use them to bring us closer to becoming a one percenter.

But the good news is that how we handle our personal goals is pretty much the same as how we handle those goals assigned to us. We just have less control over how those goals are created.

There are several factors that go into creating a valid and useful goal. The most common way of explaining these factors is to use the acronym S.M.A.R.T. or smart goals. A smart goal is a goal that meets the following criteria:

Specific

In order for a goal to be really useful, the goal itself has to be specific. It needs to be specific enough so that the person understands exactly what they need or want to do. "Try to increase sales goals" is not a valid goal. That is more of a desire or a focus item rather than a valid goal.

"Increase sales over the next 6 months by 22.5%" is a valid goal because it gives you a specific target to hit and a time period in which to hit it. Another example might be instead of "Improve my education" which is a desire and not a goal to "Complete my college degree by taking 3 courses each semester over the next two years". That is a valid goal because it is specific and leaves no doubt as to what needs to happen in order to achieve that particular objective.

Measureable

Goals also need to be measureable. IN other words, you need to be able to determine how close or far away you are to achieving a particular goal. Using the above example of "Increasing sales", without a specific figure in the goal you could say you increased sales if you sold 10,001 units this year instead of the 10,000 units you sold last year. That is still an increase but not a significant one. But if your goal was "Increase sales by 22%" and you so far have increased them 28% you know you are well on your way to hitting that year end goal. If you were at 5%, then you know you have to change something so you will get better results.

Specific measurements or values help us quickly determine whether we are heading in the right direction and how far we need to go to meet or exceed that goal. The more ways you can measure your performance the more accurate your overall results are going to be. For example, while "increase sales by 22% next year" is a valid goal, a more easily tracked goal might be "increase sales by 2% each month" or increase sales by 5.5% each quarter". This would allow you to easily track your monthly performance and make it easier to stay on track or make corrections.

Attainable

Goals are not very good if they are too not attainable.

Whatever goal you assign to yourself, it should be something that you are capable of achieving. If a goal is assigned to you by others, they should give you the tools and resources necessary you achieve those goals.

For example, "get certified in emergency planning within the next year" is an attainable goal as long as you can afford to take the course. If this is a personal goal, you would include financial planning as part of the goal. If this was assigned to you by your company, they should pay for the courses and allocate the time for you to take them and complete the work.

On the other hand "grow 6 inches by March of next year" is not a valid goal because there is no way that you can possibly control how much your body grows, if there is any growth at all, over the next year. You can eat healthy and work out and take vitamins but your body is going to grow only as much or as little as your gene tell it to grow.

Realistic

Though this can sometimes be similar to attainable, any goal that you assign yourself, or that is assigned to you, should be attainable. It should be based in reality and take into consideration all the relevant factors that might influence that goal.

For example, "grow sales by 10%" might be a realistic goal in many cases.

But if you were assigned the goal of "increase sales 4,000% next year" is most likely not an achievable goal. "Lose 10 pounds over the next 6 months" is an achievable goal for most of us. "Lose 100 pounds by next month" most certainly is not!

If your goal is realistic you can keep motivated to work towards it for longer period of time. If it is unrealistic then most of us will just look at it and not even bother to get started on it. Unrealistic goals just set up people for failure.

Timely

Dates and time frames are usually what separate goals from desires or hopes. If we have a goal with no stated time frame or deadline, then it is impossible to know whether we are on schedule or not. For example, "lose 10 pounds" might be a goal but what if you took 40 years to lose those 10 pounds? Does that mean you achieved your goal? Technically yes but that was not what you probably had in mind when you stated you wanted to lose weight. A better goal would be "Lose 10 pounds within the next 6 months." That gives you a time frame by which you can track your progress.

You should ALWAYS assign a time frame to your goals. This helps you get and stay motivated while giving you a much higher chance of completing things on schedule.

So now we know why goals are important and how they should be constructed in order to have the most impact and help us in the best way. Goals help us keep focused and motivated. Goals should be used as tools to help us get to where we want to be in life. They should also help us organize things and help us remain focused on why we are doing what we are doing. Goals help us remain focused and on track. They help us remember what has to be done and when it has to be done by. IN other words, goals help us organize our efforts and help keep them on track.

Goals also gives us easy and accurate ways to see our progress, or lack of progress, quickly and easily. This helps us understand whether we are on track or if we need a little change of attitude or focus to get back on the right road to take us where we need to go.

But the one percenters also understand that goals need not, and should not be etched in stone. They need to always reflect reality and should be modified or changed when circumstances require it. This does not give us permission to get lazy and just change a date or two. But when stuff happens, and it will, then sometimes we need to re-evaluate things and make some changes.

So now that we know why goals are important and what good goals should consist of, here are a few more points you should take into consideration when it comes to goals and how to use them:

Why One Percenters Love Goals

Goals allow us to track our progress and more fully understand what we have accomplished and how far we have come in life. Achieving a goal is a landmark moment at times and this renews our efforts, increases our confidence and better equips us to handle the demands of the future.

Goals provide us with the means of being able to push ourselves further in a measured and organized manner. Even more important, goals allow us the ability to constantly track and monitor our performance. Without having and understanding a goal, we might move in the wrong direction and not realize it for a long period of time. This means wasted time, effort and resources.

One percenters are fact driven people. They do not rely on feelings or guesses or abstract ideas in order to get where they want in life. Goals provide a fact based way of moving in an organized manner completely through a task. As you progress through the task your goals provide the constant feedback people need to become a leader or the best in their field in the shortest period of time.

One percenters also love goals because they provide a way for us to give ourselves a challenge. They give us a way to see how much we can achieve when we put our minds to it.

Assigning goals gives us the ability to sit down, analyze things and come up with ways to increase performance, improve results and become more efficient and effective at what we do.

Why You Can or Should Change Goals

The purpose of setting goals is to help us achieve more, meet deadlines or objectives and give us the ability to easily track or measure our performance against that goal. But for goals to be their most effective, and for us to get the most benefit from them, they always need to be achievable. But at the same time, they should be at least partially aggressive as well. They should "push" us to work harder or smarter. This is how we grow.

But sometimes even the most carefully and well thought out goal can be thrown into chaos by outside factors that are out of our control. This can happen to anyone for a number of reasons and we need to learn how to deal with this effectively while preserving the integrity of our goals.

I must let everyone know right now that you should not use your ability to reset or change a goal because you were lazy or didn't do anything at all. Laziness or failure to do what you were supposed to do because you just didn't get around to it is NOT a valid reason to change a goal.

If you are guilty of this type of activity, deal with it by admitting your role in the issue and commit to yourself that you will not do this again. Everyone makes mistakes and how we deal with them is important. But do not get into the habit of postponing due dates or deadlines because you decided that going to the movies was more important than getting that report done on time!

So what are some valid reasons that we all come up against?

Well, everyone gets sick every now and then and it's difficult to do your best work when you are really ill. So you might lose a day or two or even a week or more. Sometimes weather might prevent us from getting to work or work might even be forced to close for some reason. Money might become an issue when an unexpected expense might take money away from what you have to do. We all get that one once in a while. You might have to wait a month or two before you save enough money to take a course or buy some books or software or other expense you need to achieve a goal.

When these things happen, the first thing you need to do is analyze what happened and why. Then determine how these events impacted your ability to achieve your goal. How long did it delay you? Did it set you back? What was the total impact on you?

Once you understand the impact, reset your goals or time frame accordingly. For example, if the delay cost you 5 days out of work, then add 5 days to your deadline. If money issues made you lose two months, then add two months to your deadline. Do not add more time than you should. If you lose 5 days, then add 5 days not 20 days unless there is a valid reason for doing so.

There is another valid reason for resetting a goal. Sometimes we underestimate the amount of time and resources that will be needed. For example, you might think it will take you 2 days to gather information for a big report but once you start, you find out that some of the information has to be ordered and the average response time on those orders is 5 business days. Now there is no way you can complete the task in 2 days because it is going to take at least 5 days to get the information. Now you might be able to make up some time on other tasks but sometimes the difference is too great. So the only viable option is to reset the goal accordingly.

In summary, goals are not fixed in stone unless they are assigned to us by others. When we assign goals to ourselves, they should be considered "living goals" that can be changed as required. Not due to laziness or a personal failure but for valid reasons outside our control.

Changing the goal allows us to keep motivated and not get so far behind the goal no longer remains realistic or achievable. It allows us to keep focused and stay on track. After all, that is what goals are for, right?

What are Stretch Goals and Why You Should Use Them

Remember when we said that we can use goals to get us to perform at a higher level than we are currently performing or have performed in the past. When we assign ourselves goals that are designed to get us to do more than expected or more than we might be capable of, those goals are called "stretch" goals. That is because they stretch our skills and abilities and get us to learn how to do and achieve more.

Using our previous example, if your boss sets a sales goal of $1,000,000 then your stretch goal might be $1,100,000 or $1,250,000. The stretch goals is still viewed as achievable but will require more effort and for more things to go right or as planned. IN other words, if you apply yourself more to the goal you might be able to achieve your stretch goals.

Stretch goals are great because they motivate us to do more. They require us to grow our skills and abilities to a higher level than they are now. They teach us how to work under pressure and how to expect more from ourselves as well.

Stretch goals also help us with our confidence. When we achieve a stretch goal, we show ourselves that we are capable of something more than we thought we could do.

One Percenters set aggressive stretch goals for themselves because that is how you get to be the best. People who want to be the best need to perform like the best. The best require more from themselves to separate themselves from the rest of the crowd. They want to outperform everyone and be known as the best. Stretch goals allow us to learn how to be the best and expect more from ourselves.

It is also important to understand that we might not always achieve our stretch goals. After all, the stretch goal is something ABOVE what we are currently doing or what is expected. So if we fall short, it should not be thought of as a failure. In fact, it might be said that anything more than you regular goal should be considered a success because you actually did beat your regular goal.

Stretch goals are something we want to try to do because we feel we should be able to do it. They reflect where we think we should be performing and not where others think we should be. They reflect our personal feelings and desire not our actual performance.

We should always strive to do more and do better than everyone else. We should have the attitude that we can always do better and that we can always grow. That is why stretch goals can be so helpful to us.

For example, you might look at a stretch goal as a personal challenge or even a test of sorts. You might say to yourself "Ok, they want me to sell $1,000,000. I think I can sell $1,250,000 and that's what my goal is going to be this year.

Our primary focus in our goal of becoming a one percenter is to always perform at a higher level than most everyone else. In order to accomplish that goal, we need to expect more from ourselves than others expect of us. After all, no one expects someone to perform like a one percenter because many people are not capable or willing to do that.

But the one percenter to be DOES demand that from themselves because that is what they need to do in order to become what they want to be. Stretch goals help us develop the attitude and expectation we need to rise above the rest and become a one percenter. I strongly suggest you hold yourself to a higher level and that you use stretch goals to help you refine that attitude and track your progress.

All that being said, you will usually find that you have to reset or adjust stretch goals more often than regular goals. After all, you are pushing yourself and requiring that even more go exactly as planned than you did with your regular goals. So as long as you are not slacking off or being lazy, you should keep your stretch goals adjusted so they always remain achievable.

How to Prioritize Your Goals

Life would be much easier if all our goals were of equal importance and had the same urgency. But the truth all of our goals are likely to have different urgency and importance. Some might be due in two months and others in 2 hours. Some might be critical while others are on our wish list for the future.

In order to get the most from our goals, and to stand the best chance of achieving most of our goals, we need to determine the order in which we tackle each goal. This will help us get more done in less time and become more productive. It also allows us to have more control over when we do things so we can produce better and more impressive results.

One percenters understand that goals and commitments are critical to their reputation and overall success. They understand how important it is that nothing falls through the cracks, that no deadlines are missed and that no commitment is lost in the process. When any of these happens, the credibility of the individual is questioned and that is never good. So we need to do everything we can to make sure that doesn't happen.

One great way to organize your goals is by listing them on a sheet of paper or in a notebook and rank them as well. Use whatever system that works for you. For the sake of simplicity, let's say we are going to rate each goal in two ways.

The first is for urgency and the second is for importance. We will be using a rating system of 1-5 with 1 being the most urgent or important and 5 being the least urgent or important.

So, using this system, your most urgent and important goal would be ranked 1-1 while your least urgent and important goal would be a 5-5. Examples of a 1-1 might be a major report that is due today or this week. Or maybe submitting a resume for a job that will be posted tomorrow would be a 1-1 because it is so important and you want to be first.

An example of a 5-5 might be taking a course that you want to take sometime within the next 3 years. That you can do now, next month or even next year. For right now, there is little urgency and it is not that important as far as needing this done shortly.

Using this system, it is easy to glance at your list of goals and know what you should be working on now. You should update your goal sheet every week or whatever time frame works for you. Some people will update it once a day and others will do it once a month. As I said, whatever works for you.

So you update the list and then look it over. Any 1-1 goals should be your top priority. When those have been achieved you move on to the 2-2 and so on. If there are multiple goals of the same rating, then decide which you should work on first and then do the next one.

This is an easy way to keep track of your goals and to help you make sure that you get everything done before any deadlines and that you are rarely working frantically to catch up because something got lost in the shuffle.

So set your goals, keep track of them on your list, and make any adjustments that are needed to make sure those goals remain achievable and realistic. If you can manage all of this, and everyone should with a little bit of practice, you will find yourself achieving more with less stress while also experiencing more personal growth than you ever thought possible.

Shouldn't that be the goal of every one percenter?

Solve a Problem

Here is one very important way of looking at things that will help you become more successful and more in demand in your career, your industry and in life in general. Just this one little attitude adjustment can change the way you look at almost everything I life. What I want you to do is direct your efforts and views towards becoming a problem solver.

One percenters understand that the driving force behind most of the things we do or accomplish in life revolves around solving a problem. That means solving a problem or yours or a problem involving someone else. If you can be recognized as someone who will come in and solve problems, you can almost write your own ticket in life! Problem solvers are what companies and individuals look for when seeking out others!

Think about that for a moment. How much would you be in demand if a company believed you could come in and solve some of their most important problems? How much would you be worth if you could come in and innovate something to make it better, faster or cheaper? How in demand would you be by people who knew that you could make THEIR lives easier and less stressful?

One percenters understand that those people who solve problems are the highest paid and the most in demand. They understand that every single problem out there should be looked at as if it were an opportunity because that is exactly what they are! Every time someone has a problem, they search for a solution. Usually they search for someone to provide that solution.

Technicians solve problems by repairing equipment. Doctors solve problems by restoring your health and quality of life. Manufacturers create products that solve problems. They make cleaners that making cleaning easier. They make power tools that make building easier. They make beauty products that help us look better and younger and more attractive.

Every career or job revolves around solving problems as well. We hire customer service people because we need someone to handle phone calls. We hire delivery drivers because we need a way to get large products to the customer.

We need engineers to develop something that will turn an idea into reality. We need managers and supervisors to help things run smoothly and to deal with problems as they occur.

This is all important because if we focus everything we do on solving problems, we will find ourselves doing more of the things that other people want and demand. No one wants to pay someone to point out all the negatives or faults and then walk away without providing any input on how to make them any better. Yet that is exactly what a LOT of people do these days. They spend all of their time concentrating on what is wrong or bad and no time thinking about how to correct it or make it better.

Stop for a moment and think about the people you perceive as the best in their field or the most in demand. These people may very well represent the one percenters I their field. If you look closely, you will see that what they are really doing better than everyone else is providing solutions to various problems. Even more important, they are doing that better than almost everyone else.

That is why people wait for weeks for an appointment for a renowned surgeon or doctor when they could get an appointment with someone else in a couple of days. That is why people will wait for a specific contractor to do work in their house rather than go with anyone else.

Any time people are willing to either inconvenience themselves more or pay more for a service, it is because they want something better or to feel more secure.

One percenters usually charge more because they represent more. They have a reputation of being able to function at a higher level and to provide a much greater value to those who hire them. That means they are known for providing not just solutions to problems but for providing the BEST solutions!

So how do we go about providing something better than someone else does?

Well, naturally we have to be able to provide a higher level of service. That means getting the knowledge, expertise and the skills to provide a higher level of service. So if you don't have the knowledge or expertise, you need to get it. You need to get as much knowledge and expertise as possible and that knowledge needs to be current. You cannot be the best or provide the best solutions with yesterday's skills.

For the purpose of this chapter we will assume that you have the necessary knowledge, skills and expertise to provide an extremely high level of service. Now that you have all of that, you just need to channel your energy and thoughts in the right direction. That means we are ready for an attitude change.

One percenters agree that in order to be viewed as the best you have to represent yourself as being the best. That means taking your skills, expertise and abilities and presenting them to people in such a way that they are convinced that you are the very best for what they need. They cannot think you are the best one; they need to KNOW you are the best.

IN order to do this, you have to "sell" the benefits you can provide to them. You have to lead them step by step through what you can do for them and why this is so important for them. People often need to be taken by the hand and have things explained to them step. Do assume they see what you have to offer, show them. Show them why you are the best and why no one offers what you have to offer them.

Take their problems and show them how you can solve them and why your resolution is the best. Give them piece of mind and security at the same time. Show them how you have helped other people with similar problems in the past. Give them specific examples of situations where others had failed and you stepped in and solved the problem.

People all have one thing in common. They want their problems solved and they want that with as little trouble or inconvenience as possible. They will also likely be willing to pay a premium for that service as well.

Very often money or cost is not the driving factor when making a decision. Money is secondary to safety, peace of mind and security.

So whenever you try to help someone, or when you try to sell yourself or solicit someone's business, do not concentrate as much on who you are or what you can do even though all of that is important. But instead focus on how you can solve their problems better than anyone else. Show them the benefits of going with you rather than the next person. Show them how you can give them for benefits and value than anyone else can.

People sometimes get so caught up in what they can do or the features of a product they completely forget why the product or service is there in the first place! At the root of everything we do lies a problem. Look for the problem and then sell the solution not the product, person or service. Then, when the hook is set, and you have convinced the other person you are the one, then you can close the deal by talking about the services and products you represent.

This also comes in handy when you are looking to advance your career to the next level or even when you are looking for your first job in a new area or industry. Tailor your approach to target specific problems the employer might have and how you are better equipped to handle them. Even generic problems are important.

For example, everyone likes people who can show initiative and solve problems on their own. If during an interview you were to state that you believe part of your job is to handle as many issues and problems as possible so that nothing is ever passed on to your boss, that might be music to their ears especially if your next boss is the interviewer.

Or, if you were to state well known industry wide problems and how you solved them in the past that would be impressive as well. As we stated several times already, every job or position is there to perform a service or complete a task that solves a problem. So approach your interview with the idea that you are going to highlight and showcase your commitment to solving problems and providing resolutions.

I cannot stress enough how important it is to anyone looking to improve their performance or their productivity that they look at problems as mysteries looking to be solved or as opportunities. And always remember that those who solve problems are in much higher demand than those who cause them or just point them out.

Become known as a problem solver and you will be well on your way to becoming the next one percenter.

Money & Debt

Disclaimer: This chapter deals with money and how successful people handle it and think about it. This is intended as background material only. It is not intended to be used as a financial plan or for any specific recommendation for anyone. Individuals are advised to check with a financial planner or other representative before making their own decisions or plans. We assume no responsibility for financial decisions based on this information.

When it comes to success of any kind in life, people usually factor money into the equation at some point. For some people money and success go hand in hand. They just cannot see one without the other. For other people, they see success as something totally separate from money although money will still play a minor role in their definition. Regardless of how you think about money, it is something that must be considered whenever we talk about success.

The definition of a one percenter in some people's minds are the people who are among the top one percent in society when it comes to wealth. They consider the top earners or the wealthiest people as the top one percent. While our definition is much broader, and even though we consider several factors when it comes to becoming the best in anything, money still plays a vital role in the process.

Some people see money as a status symbol or an indication of how successful or powerful a person is. But money is much more than that. Money provides us with the means to get what we need and want in life. Things like food, lodging, transportation and health care all require money. Life without money today is very difficult and some might even think of it as impossible.

But what money represents for most of us is the ability to have choices in our lives. In simple terms, the more money we have the more choices we have in life. While that might not be seen as fair, it is how the world works.

For example, if I have enough money, I can afford to have other people do things for me. I can pay someone to mow the lawn for me if I hate doing it. That's my choice. I might decide to pay someone to clean my house because I either don't want to do don't have the time to do it myself. Again, that is my choice. I can eat peanut butter and jelly sandwiches because I like them not because that's all I can afford. It's my choice.

If you look at money in terms of providing more choices in life, you begin to see things differently. Everyone likes to have choices. No one wants to live or do things a certain way because they have to. They want to be able to choose the way they live. So looking at money in that regard, it just makes sense to have enough or earn enough to live the kind of life you want.

Once percenters usually see this early in life. They don't want to earn enough to just get by. They want to earn enough to live life the way they want to live it. It's not so much about possessions and fancy cars or huge houses for most people. Those are just the icing on the cake. For most people the driving force for accumulating wealth is to be able to do the things we want to when we want to.

Remember when we said that success really means being able to do more of the things we like and less of those things we dislike? Well, money enables us to do just that! Having money means choices and options and the ability to do more of the things we like and enjoy.

So how do we go about earning and getting the money we need to live our lives the way we want?

Three Ways to Have More Money

It is important to understand that there are three ways you can have more money at the end of every month or every year.

You can earn more money, spend less money or make better use of the money you have as you earn it.

Think about that for a minute. People usually feel that they need to earn more money if they want to have more money. That's just not true! If you make $80,000 a year and spend $75,000 then you have $5,000 a year left over. But if you earn $60,000 and spend $50,000 you would have $10,000 a year left over! You made less money but you had more left over because you spent less!

Most people are conditioned to spend more money that they really need to. You can buy a nice car for $20,000 yet a huge number of people will spend $35,000 and some over $100,000! There are couples who buy large houses with huge monthly payments when they need one quarter of the space!

Then there's the way we put our money to work for us. Some people put their money in a savings account earning pennies while others invest in stocks and real estate or other investments and make much more. While there is more risk, the higher return might make this more desirable.

Everyone's situation is different and it is not up to use to tell you what you should do. But be aware that there is more than one way to have more money to do the things you want in life. It is not all about earning more money. It is about what you do with your money once you earn it!

Invest in Yourself

There will be one common element in your entire life and career. That element is you. Do yourself a favor and make it a priority to invest in yourself. Take a pro-active role in preparing yourself for what lies ahead. If there is a way for you to make yourself better or more desirable to other, then invest the time and resources into doing so.

Moving forward you will be your best advocate and your best ally. What you do today and how you invest in your future will help determine how successful you are later. Never be satisfied with who you are or where you are. Invest in yourself to make yourself better. That is almost always money well spent.

Education

Well, it starts with preparation and knowledge. Knowledge comes in all shapes and forms. You get it through formal education and you get it through life experiences. The more knowledge you possess in any given field the more likely it will be that you will be prepared to take advantage of opportunities that come about later in life. So do not trivialize the value of a good education even though you feel you don't need it. You might become successful without it but your odds are greater if you have it.

Investment in education can be a very good investment if it provides you with the means of earning a larger income. But be aware that the increased cost of certain prestigious institutions might not be the smartest investment. Getting your degree is the biggest factor while where you get it might not make that much difference. In fact, for some career or jobs, a degree from just about anywhere might be sufficient.

If in doubt, check within your industry or market segment to see what is valued as far as education is concerned. For example, if you are going into the financial marketplace, a degree from Harvard is a big plus. If you are going into technology, a degree from MIT is good to have. But if you are going into other areas, a degree from somewhere else might serve you just as well.

Education is a never ending process. Truly successful people keep up with their knowledge and are constantly learning new things and updating their skills. This enables them to increase their value in the world and become more sought after and more highly compensated. You don't earn a high salary today if you have yesterday's skills.

Application

But here is something they won't teach you in any college or school. All the education in the world will do you little good if you don't use it or know how to apply it!

That means if you don't find a way to make use of what you know, or make others aware of your knowledge, it won't do you much good in life.

The one percenters and other successful people use their knowledge to turn an idea into a reality or to identify and solve serious problems. People use their knowledge to make things around us better. That is where success and prosperity come from. You give someone the ability to notice a problem and the knowledge to solve it and they will be successful if they want to be.

Attitude

Your attitude towards money will often make the difference between how well you life. If you think of money as something to be spent then you will not get the most benefit out of any money you get. In order to make the most out of your money it needs to be saved, invested and planned for. Your attitude must always be long-term and never short-term unless it is about reducing debt.

You should always plan on saving money for medium and long range expenses. Medium expenses include purchasing a house, buying a car, and planning for growth. Long range expenses would include saving for retirement, paying for your children's education and for long term medical care.

You must never feel that if you have $500 in your hands you have $500 to spend. Always save a percentage of your income for medium and long range expenses. Pay yourself that first and then use what's left over. You would be shocked to see know how many people fail to grasp this simple strategy!

Good Debt & Bad Debt

There is a myth out there that any kind of debt is bad debt. Well that is just not the case. There are some things in life that it makes sense to go into debt for if the circumstances are right. Examples would include purchasing a home instead of renting if you can get a good interest rate and a good price on a suitable home. Another example might be borrowing money to start your own business if you have a good and reasonable idea and a good business plan.

Those are examples of good debt because those expenses will pay for themselves over time. Your home will go up in value and your business will hopefully provide a lifetime of good income for you.

Bad debt would include taking out a loan to go on vacation, taking out a large car loan for an expensive luxury car or taking out any loan for something you do not absolutely need and can't do without. You do need food but you do not need filet mignon.

You do need a roof over your head but that roof doesn't need to be a mansion on the hill. Any debt for these things that requires you to spend over your limits should be considered bad debt.

Any debt that does not provide you with a benefit moving forward should be seriously considered and eliminated. If it isn't "good debt" then it should be "no debt"!

Credit Card Debt

One perfect example of really bad debt is credit card debt. While credit cards are almost required in life today, we should be careful when using them and make every effort to pay off the balance in full to avoid interest rates as high as 30% a year! Would you go to a store and buy something if their "sale" was a price increase of 30%? Of course you wouldn't! But that is what you are doing when you pay credit card interest on your purchases or on that vacation!

Every penny you pay in interest is one penny less that you will be able to use for other purchases. Managing your debt is absolutely critical if you want to get the most out of your money for now and in the future. If you are saddled with large amounts of debt you may never be able to climb back out of it.

If you must incur debt, always look for sources of money at the lowest possible interest rate.

Roll over credit card debt into low interest loans to cut your interest payments. But that will only work if you stop adding to your debt by running up more credit card debt in the future.

If you can pay off your balance in full and avoid finance charges, take advantage of cards that offer rebates or airline miles based on your purchases. This can save you hundreds of dollars a year on purchases and airfares. But again, this only works in your favor if you pay off everything in full every month. Otherwise, the high interest easily overcomes any rewards benefits.

Budget Your Money

Here is another are where most people fall way short when it comes to managing their money. Everyone should have a budget. Everyone should know what their fixed expenses are and how much they spend every week or month. You cannot possibly manage money properly if you don't know what you bring in and what you spend every week.

One percenter and other successful people will have a great grasp on what they spend and where their money goes. They know how much money they can safely and responsibly spend on something before they buy it and not afterwards! They are able to make informed decisions on what should be spent before they buy things and not later!

Spend Within Your Limits

Everyone should live within one basic premise. That is that we should live within our means and purchase things within our income. That means buying appropriate things for the money we earn. It makes no difference what your friends or next door neighbors buy. You should only buy what you can afford and nothing more.

That means buying a used car if you cannot afford a new one. It means living in a smaller house that you can afford instead of that 12 room 4 bath house on the bluff. Don't let anyone tell you that you are entitled to anything in life when it comes to possessions. You are entitled only to what you can afford! Convincing you otherwise is the goal of every salesman out there. If you can't afford it, do not buy it!

In the beginning this might be difficult. But instead of going into debt, one percenters use this as motivation to go out and get a better job or earn a better living. One percenters will do what they need to do in order to be able to afford the things they want in life. They do not buy things because they want them. They buy things they can afford instead.

Walk Away from Impulse Purchases

We all have times when we see something we want, or we listen to a sales pitch, and we are tempted to go ahead and buy something.

The problem with that is sometimes we wind up buying things we either don't need, we pay too much for them, or we discover too late it really was a stupid decision in the first place. It is usually a much better idea to walk away and take some time to think about it before you make the purchase.

Beware of salesmen who tell you that their offer is only good for the next 15 minutes or if you walk out the door you won't get the same offer later. If they try that just leave immediately and don't make the purchase. There is a reason they tell you that. They don't want to give you the opportunity to investigate of check things out to see what a poor deal it really is. Or maybe you could buy the same exact thing elsewhere for half the price.

Always take some time, preferably a day or so, to think things through. You might even want to ask someone else's opinion or check with your financial advisor. It is always better to be safe instead of sorry. If it is truly the right thing to do the sale will be there tomorrow. Even if it isn't, it will be on sale again in the future. Remember, for every legitimate deal offered with a time limit there are hundreds of bad deals offered in the same manner using the same sales pitch.

Consider a Financial Planner

This is not a book on money management and I don't pretend to know anything more than the basics of how to use and manage money. There are a ton of ways to get more out of your money and how you can be responsible with the money you have. I think everyone should at least consult with a financial planner at a few critical stages of their life.

They should consult with a financial planner at the beginning of their career so they get in the habit of treating money properly and using it responsibly. You can also start retirement accounts and start retirement saving at an earlier age as well.

Then when you get established in your career or when you start a family you should start planning for those additional expenses as well. College savings, changes to retirement planning, life insurance and other financial matter can be effectively planned for at this time.

Later on as you get a bit older and when the kids are older, you might want to consider addressing your older age and health care and retirement savings. Check to make sure you are on track to be where you want for retirement and that you have arranged for health care and possibly long term care as well. These expenses can drain even the largest retirement savings accounts.

Plan for Retirement

I read in an article a few weeks ago that over 50% of people have less than $20,000 in retirement savings and that most people approaching retirement age have less than $50,000 in total savings. These are the same people who still are carrying mortgage and other debt into retirement as well.

You cannot expect to live a happy and comfortable life in retirement without significant retirement savings. With life spans growing longer and longer as medical care gets better and better; more people are running out of money during their retirement than ever before.

Remember what we said earlier when we said that having money gave you more options in life. Never is this more relevant than when it comes to retirement. When you are 20 and you needed extra money you could grab some overtime or take a second job. You might have even been able to land a second job. When you are 80 years old those options are pretty much gone.

Do yourself a favor and start planning for your retirement as early as possible. Starting younger means your money will grow with interest for longer periods of time. The earlier you start the less you will have to put away each month and still have a nice retirement portfolio. Do not put off saving for retirement whatever you do.

Be Careful About Greed

One percenters and other successful people understand that when something sounds so good that it can't possibly be true then it probably isn't true. Ponzi schemes, real estate fraud, suspicious low or high interest rates should always be red flags to you.

It makes sense to realize that if everyone else is paying 5% and someone tells you he can get you 30%, then something just isn't right. The same thing holds true for "sure thing" stock tips and other so-called opportunities.

Always be aware that there are people in this world whose sole goal is separating you from your hard earned money. Always protect your money and only invest it in legitimate opportunities with well known and trusted institutions. Even then, do your homework and make sure everything looks, sounds and feels right. If something isn't for you, just walk away.

Diversify

One percenters and successful people understand the need to invest their money in several different places and types of investments. You should never put all your money in one place, in one stock or in one kind of investment. Things can go wrong in any company or with any one stock and you would not want to lose everything by having all your money in that one area.

There are many different types of investments including bonds, stocks, stock funds, mutual funds and other funds. Add to that investment accounts, IRA's and other options and you should be able to create a diversified portfolio that will give you a decent return on your investment while keeping you safe at the same time.

Keep in mind that investment companies want you to invest as much money in their products as possible and they will advise you accordingly. With that in mind, it might be wise to consult with a financial planner before committing to any one investment or creating your portfolio.

Summary

Successful people look at money as a tool to use to make sure they live the life they want to lead. As we stated several times, money gives us options. It gives us the ability to do what we want and to have others do the things we don't want to do ourselves. But that only works when we get the most out of our money and use it properly.

We should also let you know that there is just one person who is responsible for your money. That is you. Even though you might consult or hire a professional to monitor you money for you, you are still the one responsible for your money. Make smart decisions and manage your money carefully. If you do hire someone else to manage it for you, ask a lot of questions and ask for updates frequently. If you have any money is something you don't understand, ask them about it. If it doesn't sound right, remove it. If your advisor doesn't feel right, find another one who makes you feel more secure.

Most people who are out to cheat you thrive on certain people not caring about knowing what is happening with their money. These people do what benefit them and the next thing you know your savings or retirement funds are gone and you are left with nothing. While there is nothing you can do to protect yourself 100% of the time, asking questions and being knowledgeable will go a long way towards keeping your investments safe and secure.

The key is getting the most from your money and saving a portion of it now so it will be allowed to work for you later on. So earn today and invest in tomorrow. That is what one percenters do and you should start learning about today.

The Extra Effort

Sometimes the most effective things you can do are the easiest. When it comes to becoming successful, and eventually a one percenter, there is one easy thing you can train yourself to do that will provide almost instant results. That one thing is being willing to put in the extra effort needed to produce better results than anyone else.

We live in a society where more emphasis is placed on speed and cost than is placed on the quality of the results we get from our efforts. If we get it done fast, and we get it done cheaper, that's good enough. Well, it's good enough for some but it shouldn't be good enough for you.

Think about the time you have worked during your life. If you are young then think about the people you know at school. Whether at school or at work we all know people who do just enough to get by.

They are satisfied with mediocre results and barely passing grades. They might even make fun or, or look down at, those who produce better results or get higher grades. Either way, they don't demand much of themselves.

These are the people who produce presentations that are "OK" but nothing impressive. These are the people that do what is asked of them but not a single thing more, even if something a little extra might make a huge difference. In school it was the student who was happy with the 71 because they passed the course.

We don't want to approach life like these people do. We need to have more respect for ourselves than that. We need to learn to expect our best efforts no matter the task or situation. We need to expect to do a little extra when it's needed to produce a much better result. We do this not because it is demanded of us but because we understand the value in doing it.

That might mean inserting charts and graphics into a presentation to impress a client and land a new account. It might mean studying a little bit more to get a 90 on a big test instead of a 75. It might mean adding an extra hour of work in order to make the result better, clearer and more impressive. Whatever the reason might be, we do it because we see the reason to do it. We don't need to be told to do it we just do it.

We spoke before about life and careers being competitions. In any competition it is not the second of third best person who wins. It is the BEST person that wins. It is the fastest runner or swimmer. The highest scorer wins the scoring title not the one who scored the second most points. The best salesman is not the one who sold the third most products. It's the one who sold the most.

No one remembers the runners up in life. At least not most of the time. Honorable mention is nice but reputations are not built on being OK. They are built by excelling and becoming the best. That means putting in the time and work to be the best. In short, it means putting in the extra effort!

Actually, training yourself to be that way is not all that hard. All you have to do is ask yourself whenever you are doing something if there is anything else you could do to make something better? Should it be re-read another time to see if better word choices could be made? Can you add content or graphics to a presentation to make it look and flow better? Could you have done more preparation or gathered more information?

Preparation is often the area where most people fail or at least come up short. Gathering of information or researching something is not the most enjoyable or glamorous part of any task. But often this is where huge differences are made.

Going the extra mile in the beginning can give you information that could give you an advantage that might be a game changer. So always ask yourself if you should have prepared more or if there is anything else that is needed to make something complete.

For example, let's talk about the candidate who arrives at an interview with little or no knowledge about the company he is interviewing with. He answers questions well using generic answers. His answers are good but not overly relevant or specific. He is knowledgeable but doesn't really come across that way because he knew almost nothing about the company. He didn't do his preparation very well.

Contrast that to the next candidate who researched the company and looked into what they were looking for in this particular position. His answers are crisp and complete and he used specific examples and references that were directly relevant to that same company. He is knowledgeable and comes across as knowledgeable because he knew about the company and their needs.

Who do you think would come off as the superior candidate? Who do you think would get the job offer?

This is so simple yet many people do not bother to go the extra mile or put in the extra effort.

That means those people who do will have an immediate and considerable advantage over those people. It's like starting a race and stopping to tie your shoes after the starting gun sounds. You're still in the running but you are so far behind you have to hope someone else falls or you will never catch up.

Successful people and one percenters don't do things where they need to hope someone else messes up so they can succeed. They step up and do the things that help them look like the best and enable them to eventually be the best. If the boss asks for A&B they give him A,B,C & D. If they client expects A, B and C, they will throw in D, E, and F in as well. Not because they have to but because they will impress others if they do that.

We need to go through our lives and career with the attitude that we are going to try and be the best at everything we do. We need to act in that manner as well. We want to do whatever we can to make others respect and admire us. Speaking of respect, there is one important thing you should know right now.

People don't demand respect. People are not automatically entitled to respect either. While we should treat everyone with respect, we do not have to respect them as a person. Respect is earned not demanded.

So the right phrase should be "People command respect." In other words, people respect you for who you are and what you have done and also how you did it. Results are important but it is also important how you got those results.

People who are known for putting in the extra effort are respected among their peers and throughout their industries. These are the people others come to for help, advice and partnerships. These are the people who are exposed to the most opportunities and who have the most options in life.

So you have a choice to make. Do you want to be the one who puts in the extra effort and gets further ahead in life or are you going to be content by staying in the rest of the pack?

In other words, are you going to strive to be a one percenter or a 99 percenter?

The choice is yours.

Work Efficiently

One percenters understand the need to get things done well but also get them done fast. They understand that in most cases, time is money and it is important to be among the leaders or the first people to get something finished. They understand success is a competition and those who use their resources and skills better are often the winners.

One percenters also understand that the one great equalizer no matter who you are, how much you earn or where you work is that everyone just gets 24 hours a day. No one gets more and no one gets less. So it is not so much how much time you have it's what you do with that time that really counts.

If that makes sense to you, and it should, then you should also agree that there are two ways to get more done in the same period of time.

You can either work harder or you can work smarter. Because no one really wants to work harder, it just makes sense that it is better to work smarter or more efficiently. That is not because we are lazy; it is because it is better to work smarter.

So what exactly does work smarter mean and why is it the best way to work?

Working smarter means working in such a manner that you don't waste time, you don't make mistakes and that you do things in the most efficient manner possible. When you adopt this approach you get more done in less time with less stress and usually with much better results. Working smarter also means being organized and doing things more efficiently and with better work flow.

Working smarter usually means creating a system or method of working that enables you to get more done with less effort and in less time. That means coming up with a process that works for you. The process usually takes several things into consideration and provides the best overall work environment possible for you to function in. That means everything in its place and everything you need available when and where you need it.

This might sound impossible or at least very complicated but here are a few things to help you get started working smarter and more efficiently:

Organization

The basic key to working efficiently is learning how to become organized. While you do not have to be over zealous when it comes to organization, you do have to create some kind of system that allows you to find things you need when you need them without wasting time hunting around for them.

That means assigning a place for certain things and then keeping things in that one place. You should not have 4 different places for storing reports, tools, data, or other things. Reports should all be stored together and tools should be stored together. If you have tools stored in 4 different locations you stand to have to look in all 4 places before you find what you need. This wastes time and resources that could have been used to work on the task at hand.

You also need to store things in an organized manner. If you have all your reports thrown in one box and every time you need something you have to leaf through the entire box, that wastes time as well. Separating things into sub folders or drawers can be helpful.

The same thing applies with tools as well. Keep like tools in the same tool box or cabinet. If you keep things together you will quickly be able to see if you have a particular tool and decide whether or not you need to go out and buy one.

If they are misplaced or stored all around the place you may waste time and resources going out to purchase something you already own!

You also need to organize the things you need to do. The ability to know what needs to be done by which date and in what order can help you avoid deadline crunches and other problems. Being able to organized tasks so what needs to be done before other tasks is handled with ease and accuracy.

The goal is to be able to find things when you need them and have things ready for when you need them as well. This way there are no down periods while you are waiting for something to be completed. You move seamlessly from one step to another.

Working in this fashion not only saves time but it keeps your focus and thought flow intact as well. This enables you to keep on going without having to stop to think where you were, what you were thinking and where you need to start back up from.

Resource Allocation & Utilization

In order to work efficiently we have to be aware of the resources that we have available to us and how we are going to use them. We need to have easily accessible information that lets us know who to contact for what reason.

We should know who does what and other information that is pertinent to using them. For example, what is the lead time they require to do a certain kind of work? How do you contact them? How much do they cost? This will enable us to quickly determine who is the best choice and what the time frames are likely going to be. Having this information ready at a moment's notice will help increase the work flow and allow us to make the best choices and make them fast and accurately.

Work Flow

Successful people understand the importance of doing things in a logical and orderly manner. That means doing things in the correct order so everything is done without waiting or interruption.

For example, you cannot write the conclusion to a book before you write the main content of the book. You cannot write the report first and gather the information needed to write the report second. You need to design the work flow so that everything needed for a particular step in the process is there waiting for you.

This is not difficult once you get the hang of creating work flow. The easiest way is to write down each task that needs to be done and then the steps or requirements of each task.

Then look at everything and list things in the correct order so that the preceding steps give you everything you need for the current step.

If everything is done properly, you will flow from one step to the next all the way through to completion. There should be no gaps, no waiting for something and wasting time and everything should proceed in an orderly manner. There might be a "blip" or two at times but you can usually deal with those easily. Focus on the flow as you expect it and you should be fine.

Prioritizing

We talked about this before but it bears repeating in the context of working smarter and more efficiently. If you want to truly work effectively, you need to be able to control your deadlines and responsibilities so you do as much work on your schedule as possible.]

We all have times of the day when we do our best work and our worst work. Maybe we are morning people or night people. It stands to reason that when we work during times that are best for us that we will accomplish more with better results. We can only do this when we are able to decide what we work on and when we work on it.

That is why being able to prioritize what we do is so important. Being able to get things done before they are due gives us the flexibility we need to work better and with less stress. We should never wait until the last minute or forget about things until it is too late.

We must always make an effort to do the most important and most urgent tasks first and then tackle everything else. Doing thing this way will enable us to have more control over what we do and how we do it.

Delegation

One things one percenters understand is that they do not have to do everything themselves. No matter how skilled and talented a person might be, there are always other people who are better at certain tasks than they are. These are people who can provide much better results and often do so in shorter periods of time. It would not only be foolish not to use those people, it would be outright stupid!

One of the keys to success is doing more of what you are truly good at and delegating everything else to people who are good at those tasks. This way you get more done and create more value to either the company or your efforts. You save time in the process as well.

Think about a project where you have to write ad copy, design a website, create physical advertising and design packaging. That means 4 tasks need to be completed before the project can be finished and placed in the marketplace.

Now you might be capable of doing all 4 tasks and you might be able to do a decent job on all 4 as well. But if you had 3 other people each specially skilled and experienced in the other 3 tasks, the group could work on all 4 tasks simultaneously and save a ton of time. The product gets to market earlier, the advertisements are written and designed better, the website looks great and works create and the packaging really catches the eyes of the customers.

So not only have you completed the project faster and placed the product on the shelves earlier, every part of the process was done better and faster as well. Different people using their own specialized skills accomplished more in less time and everything was done with better results. How can you argue with that?

Successful people know it is not smart to try and do everything yourself. They understand that speed is sometimes critical and anything that can be done to speed up the process while getting better results is the best way to go. If you have the resources and are able to use them, there is no better way to go.

So why do some people resist delegating work to others?

There are several reasons. The main one is that some people have huge egos. They tell themselves that no one can possibly do a better job because they are so skilled and so wonderful. We all know that's a load of crap but they don't see it that way.

Ego also gets into play when someone feels that this is their project, their idea and their legacy. They are so interested in taking total credit that they lose sight of what is in the product or projects best interests. If they had been confident and objective enough to see things in reality, there would be no question that they should delegate tasks to qualified individuals.

Another reason is sometimes, especially in the early stages of a business or career you do not have access to well qualified people. This can be a problem. In these cases you must outsource this work and that can cost money you might not have.

Another reason to keep things to yourself might very well be a valid one. Secrecy can be a powerful reason not to give anyone access to a project or product until the very last minute. If you outsource or share packaging or advertising, someone else might steal your idea or concept and beat you to the marketplace. That can be a real concern and it needs to be carefully thought about.

But if secrecy is not a concern and you do have access to personnel and resources, make good use of them.

It will enable things to get done faster and better and lower your workload and stress levels at the same time. There is very little to argue with there!

Some one percenters will take this concept to the extreme. They will come up with the basic ideas or concepts and then let other people turn them into reality while they work on the next idea or concept. This means their work is focused on what they do best while others function in the support roles. As long as everyone is doing what they are best at, delegation is usually the best strategy when it comes to doing more in less time.

Taking Care of Yourself

All the success in the world will not do you much good if you are not around to enjoy it. All the money in the world doesn't matter to you if you cannot enjoy it or spend it. You can leave it to friends and relatives but was that your plan when you earned it? I sincerely doubt that. The fact is, if we don't take care of ourselves, very little else matters. We need to be priority one.

One percenter and other successful people understand the need to take the steps they need to take to keep themselves in good health. That means keeping themselves in good conditioning and getting the exercise they need. They also understand the importance of good nutrition and stress control.

Building a career or become a one percenter is not all that easy. If it were, everyone would do it and it would lack the prestige that being the best carries with it. But along with the work comes pressure and stress. How we deal with that stress is important and critical to overall success and achievement.

Another part of health that has a direct impact on what we do and how we do it is our energy levels. It stands to reason that if we feel good we will be able to do more, concentrate longer and stay motivated. If we have the energy we need to get through the day we will become more productive and more proficient as well.

For example if you are in poor condition and you get tired by noontime and need a 3 hour nap. Others are likely going to be able to accomplish more in one day than you are. If you get tired early and cannot concentrate, your results will suffer as well. So let's just agree that our ability to function throughout the day is paramount to our overall success!

First and foremost, we encourage everyone to keep their health in tip top shape. That means yearly physicals, smart eating and exercise and an overall healthy lifestyle. While we are not doctors, we do suggest you see your doctor for any health related issues and for whatever reasons you might have. Your health affects everything in your life and it should be your top priority.

One area we are going to discuss in detail is stress and its role in your health and in your success. Everyone has stress in their lives and most of us handle it quite well. We are used to it and we just deal with it. But when stress levels get too high, they affect the body in negative ways. That presents a very real problem for some of us.

Stress is present whenever we are exposed to anything that is not something we are comfortable with or anything that takes us out of our comfort zone. It also is around when we ask or expect our bodies to do something to excess or when we just ask it to do too much. Unfortunately, this can happen frequently throughout our lives. Since we cannot eliminate stress, we need to know how to deal with it.

There are many ways to deal with stress. But the most effective way to deal with stress is to create a lifestyle that contains less stress to begin with. Here are some suggestions to reduce stress and help keep us healthy:

Watch Your Workload

Expecting our minds and bodies to work constantly over long period of time is just asking for trouble. The mind and body need some "downtime" so they can rest and heal themselves. While an occasional "all nighter" is fine when needed, constantly working long hours with little to no rest is very stressful and very hard on the body.

Moderation is the key along with frequent breaks. Take a short walk around the building to get the blood flowing. If you work at home and feel stressed, try a 30 minute "power nap" or go for a walk to get refreshed a bit.

Rest a Bit!

Listen to your body. When the body feels tired it is telling us that it needs some rest. While we don't have to listen to it all the time, we should be aware of the signs that we are doing too much or working too long. Listen and pay attention and give your mind and body rest when they need it.

Everyone needs a good night sleep on a regular basis. Make sure that you get what your body needs in the way of sleep. For most of us 7-8 hours is considered normal. But if you require a little more or less, try and get it whenever you can. Short naps during the day are not the same as deep sleep. Create a schedule that lets you get the sleep you need.

Take a Walk

Walking is a form of low impact cardio exercise and this can rejuvenate you and make you feel better. It helps get the blood flowing and it reduces stress as well. In fact any kind of exercise will help you lose some of the built up stress in your body.

Hit the Gym

If stress is higher than you would like, consider hitting the gym for a workout. Lifting weights or using the equipment for a vigorous workout will really help you melt the stress away. Be sure to check with your doctor before you start any exercise program. Doing too much too soon is never a good thing. Make sure you start slow and gradually build up your workout.

Be Pro-Active

Remember when we said that those who develop a pro-active attitude have less stress in their lives? Well any time we can do things on our schedule or at our convenience means less stress. Working without a deadline hanging over our heads is easier and less stressful than having to work hard to get something done quickly.

Let Little Things Go

This one might be a little hard to do for some of us. If you really want to reduce the stress in your life then learn to let some of the little things go in life. Don't worry about little things that really have little effect on life.

If your son left his dirty socks on the floor instead of yelling at him and getting upset, just throw them in the hamper. If someone doesn't share your passion for being perfect, cut them some slack.

We are all different and we need to develop some tolerance with each other.

If you look at things at a higher level you will see that things are really not that bad. In fact, you will probably find they are much better than you really thought!

Listen to Your Body

The human body is a wonderful thing. It can heal itself and it can protect you against disease and illness. But it has its limits and it will tell you when enough is enough. If something hurts or feels different, it's your body's way of telling you that something isn't right.

If you pull a muscle it hurts so you will be reminded to rest it a little and give it a chance to heal. As it heals the pain subsides to let you know it's OK to go back to normal. If you feel tired or exhausted your body is telling you that you need more rest. If you get a headache your body might be telling you that you are reading too much or using your brain too much. You need to listen to what your body is telling you.

Sometimes your body takes matters into its own hands. It will make you feel bad in order to force you to rest. Headaches, aches and pains, and cold like symptoms force you to dial things back a little and rest.

Some people feel that frequent colds or aches and pains are the body's way of telling you to slow down a little. As I said, listen to your body and what it is telling you.

Plan in Stages

Do you know what you want out of life? Even more important, do you know how to go about getting what you want? Our needs and goals will change over our lifetime. What we wanted in our 20's is not likely going to be the same as what we want in our 60's! So we must know what we want to accomplish now to help us prepare for later.

If you want to be the best, you need a plan on how to get there. You need a plan for now and you need a plan for later as well. In fact there are several stages we need to plan for. Successful people understand that they need to have some idea of where they want to be at certain times in their future. Just like you wouldn't start a cross country trip without a map, you shouldn't go through life without a plan!

With that in mind, here are some stages of life that you should be planning for. Remember that each stage of your plan must adequately prepare you for the next stage. The goals and needs for each stage are likely to be different. We will concentrate on our career for our examples but keep in mind the same holds true for your personal life as well.

Here are some of the stages you might want to plan for in life:

Planning for Your Career

When you are younger, or whenever you plan on making a major change in life, you need to think things through and figure out some new goals or deadlines to make sure you get where you want to go in an organized and timely manner.

There are usually some questions that should be asked before making any move such as "Why do I want to do this?" "Is now the right time for this? "Is this a smart decision?" These types of questions are designed to have you think things through so you don't do something foolish in your life like quit your $200,000 a year job to open a snow cone stand in Alaska!

But if what you want to do has some valid reasons behind it, and you have the time and resources to do things right, then what you need to plan for now is how to get through the period of adjustment that always accompanies a major change. Issues like how you will support yourself while you are learning or working at a lower paid position in your new career. This might not be an issue but it is something that needs to be asked.

The most important information you might need at this point is whether there is a market for the type of career you are thinking about entering. It should be something we enjoy and get pleasure out of but it also needs to be something that has a reasonable future and considerable job opportunities. This is important to know before you commit to the change because you do not want to invest time and a lot of money into learning and preparing only to find out there are no jobs available when you are ready.

You also need to find out what qualifications you will need to get started. What are employers looking for in new hires? What do you need to do to prepare yourself for this new career or opportunity? How long is it going to take for you to prepare? What costs are involved? All of these things need to be understood before you make any change.

The Start of Your Career

Now that you have started a new career or job, or maybe even started your own business, you should also create a rough plan on where you expect to be career-wise over the next few years and beyond. How do you think your want the growth in your career to happen and what should your career be in 5 years or 10 years from now?

What goals have you set for salary or business growth over the next 5 to 10 years? How do you expect to achieve those goals? What things do you have to do to prepare and qualify for a higher position? What do you plan to do to increase your perceived value? Do you plan on takings classes, get a certification or anything along those lines?

Growing Your Career

As you continue in a current career, or whether you are still operating your own business, you need to think about the future and how you are going to go from where you are now to where you WANT to be in 10 or 15 years from now. Do you have any specific goals or dreams? If you do, try and figure out a timeline for where you would like to be to position yourself for that better job.

For example, if you are planning for a manager's job, your plan might include taking some management courses, getting the required certification and volunteering your time and expertise in order to increase visibility.

Whatever you can think of that will help you better prepare for what comes next will serve you well and help you achieve your goals.

Establishing Your Professional Image

If you are really going to become a one percenter, you will have to create a professional image that helps set you apart from everyone else. This requires careful planning and scheduling because this process is going to take some time.

Create a plan by first listing all the ways you can create a great reputation and make yourself known in the industry and in your area. Write down everything you can. Nothing is too small. Also write down specific ideas you have that will make you look great at the same time.

Now take all of that information and ideas and put them in the right order and assign some deadlines for each item or group of items. List things you can start on today and then items you will work on for next year and beyond. The idea is to know what needs to happen and then being aware of when you need to do all of these things in order to create a great reputation.

Becoming an Expert

Training for a career or job is pretty much the easy part.

You take classes, you do some on the job training, and you learn from your experiences. This might take you 6 months or it might take 6 years. But for most careers there is a well thought out plan for getting the education and skills you need to succeed.

But when you strive to exceed what most other people know, then it sometimes can get more difficult. You will have to seek out ways to learn more, experience more and contribute more to the process. This usually means taking seminars, advanced level courses and joining groups and organizations that will provide the knowledge and expertise usually not shared with others. All this takes time and effort.

You might decide to teach others about what you do in order to establish yourself as an expert. Whatever plans you have to establish yourself as an expert you need to write them down and assign a timeframe for each one. Time is important. Establishing yourself as an expert early in your career will bring you much more money and prestige than it would if you established yourself as an expert when you turned 70!

Transitioning into Retirement

As we get later on in life, at some point we slow down on the growth part of our career and we look further ahead towards the future.

We might "rest" a little on our reputation and cut back on our workload as well. After all, we have worked hard to get where we are and it's time to enjoy things a bit.

At this point we start thinking about our retirement and how we want to spend our later years. Do we want to (or have to) work part-time in our retirement? Do we have any goals or dreams we want to fulfill during retirement?

The time to start thinking about this is not when you are 64. This should be thought about when you turn 50 or so or even earlier for some. This is important because the things we want to do will affect the amount of money we will likely need for retirement. Even if we started saving in our 20's (which I am sure you did!) you might find that you have to put away a little more over the next 10-15 years to retire comfortably. It's better to discover that now instead of when it is too late!

Retirement & Beyond

Everyone needs to give some thought about how life is going to be when you get older and head into retirement. There will be health issues to contend with at some point and those will cause financial issues as well. It is shocking how many people have no idea what they will need or what they should do until it is too late.

Everyone who is retired or close to retirement should make two important visits. The first is to a financial planner to get an opinion and some guidance on how they should manage their retirement savings. Issues like health care and long term care should be discussed if they already haven't been.

Your lawyer can help you protect your assets and savings through setting up trusts and creating your will if you don't already have them. There are ways to protect your savings and isolate them from health care expenses and other problems our seniors often have. Do not feel you are immune to these problems or that you have enough money to handle anything. You shouldn't feel that way because you probably don't have enough money to handle certain situations.

It is better to be safe than sorry and you can give yourself peace of mind while protecting your hard earned savings. While the two visits will cost you a few dollars, you will get much more back in security and the preservation of your assets.

When Plans are no Good!

I hope we can agree that planning for the different stages that we go through in life is a smart idea. Having an idea of where you want to be at any given time gives us a way to judge our progress at a glance.

We read our plan, look at the dates, and compare that to where we are. Hopefully we are right on schedule or maybe ahead of schedule a bit. Both of those are just fine.

But if we look at our plan and we are behind schedule, we might need to change our approach or re-focus on what needs to be done. We might even have to change our plans as life changes and things outside of our control change as well. The important thing is to not focus on assigning blame but rather on what it will take to get us back to where we want to be. Our plan will make that much easier.

But sometimes having a plan will not do us one bit of good. You know when that happens? That happens when you take the time and effort to create an excellent plan that covers everything and gives you a clear path to follow. Then you take that plan and place it in a folder or drawer and never take it out or consult it ever again!

In order for any plan to work, it has to be followed, updated, adjusted and worked constantly. While you don't have to consult it every day, you should pull it out at least a couple of times each year to see how you are doing. At that time you can either pat yourself on the back or kick yourself in the butt depending on how well you did.

Think of your plan as a wall on either side of the path you need to go down in life. The more you focus and use your plan the higher the walls get on each side of you.

Those walls help guide you down the right path. The higher the walls the more difficult it will be to stray off the path. The shorter those walls are, the easier it becomes to step to the side and go the wrong way.

Plans are a process that needs to be followed. Designing your plans is just the first step. Once you design them, you follow them. If you stray off course, the more often you check your plan the fast you will be able to get back on course.

Your plan is never really done. You will leave some steps behind as you move on but there will always be things to do, decisions to be made and more plans for the future. So make you plan, work your plan, and enjoy your life.

Creating Balance

Here is one concept that most one percenters and other successful people totally grasp. That is the concept of creating balance in your life. That means taking all of the different parts of life and making sure to include each one in our weekly activities. Creating balances means taking the time to give everything some attention and not paying all your attention to just one part of life.

One percenters are generally extremely committed to their careers. After all, no one gets to the top without putting in the time and effort and sacrifice along the way. If you could make it to the top without all of those things, the top would be a very crowded place! There is no problem with being focused and committed. The problem is when that focus and commitment takes precedence over everything else in life.

For the average person, the different parts of their lives might include family, friends, career, health, hobbies, relaxation, spiritual, love and relationships. You might have other parts of your life as well but these are among the most common. All of these different parts of our life help us to live happy and fulfilled lives that are rewarding as well.

The problem arises when any one or two of these areas takes over all of our thoughts and efforts. When this occurs our lives become unbalanced. That means that some areas of our life are being shut out or neglected. When this happens problems occur and the overall quality of our life is lowered.

When someone is so focused on their job or career, or when their job and career place extreme demands on their time and efforts, an unbalanced lifestyle occurs. There might be no time for family and friends, you might be too busy to start a relationship or give proper attention to a current relationship. Those areas suffer and sometimes permanent damage can occur. You might lose a close friend or have to end a relationship. You might create hard feeling within your family because you are too busy to attend important family functions or holiday gatherings. Whatever the repercussions might be, they are all negative as far as you are concerned.

For example, if you want to become a one percenter and you are focused on that and only that, you might make commitments to do so much and spend so much time learning and working and volunteering that you ignore everyone and everything else in your life. You are working 100 hours a week and the rest of the time you are taking classes. After all, you want to be the best and you are willing to do whatever it takes to become the best.

While that kind of commitment is admirable on its face, it requires a level of action and focus that really is not sustainable without causing serious damage to the other parts of life. That is why creating a balanced lifestyle is so important. You can work long hours and you can be career driven, you just have to make room for others things as well.

Another reason for creating balance in your life is to avoid burnout. Burnout occurs when you do something for too long and at too high a level. Most of us can easily walk a mile without getting tired or winded. Heck, most of us walk between 5,000 and 10,000 steps a day without even thinking about it. That's roughly 2-4 miles!

But if we try and run full speed for even half a mile most of us would pass out on the street from fatigue! We just cannot sustain such vigorous activity for long period of time.

For short bursts, we can run full speed. For longer distances we have to pace ourselves. Otherwise we burn out and we are forced to quit.

We can eliminate burnout by dialing back either the intensity or the duration of what we are doing and replacing some of that time with other activities. We can take that 100 hours a week and dial it back to 75 hours and spend some of that time with family and friends or just relaxing. We can stop working late every night and cut it back to every other night and use the extra time to get a full night's sleep several nights a week.

I can hear some of you saying that if we cut off 25 hours of work each week things will take longer to do and we might miss out on some things because of that. You won't be ready or you'll fall behind or someone else will beat you to the marketplace. Well, all of that is true but it's not as bad as you might think. That is because you will be replacing quantity with quality.

When you stop working long hours and give your body and mind a chance to heal and recover, you can spend those remaining hours of work performing at a higher level and achieving better results. You will be rested and better able to focus and remain focus instead of drifting off and zoning out half the time.

Balance in life is important for another reason as well. Very few people can live in seclusion in this world. We all need to be around other people and have social and business interaction. That is how we learn and grow and it is what brings fulfillment and satisfaction into our lives. In simpler terms, life is much nicer and more rewarding when we have someone to share it with.

All the money in the world will not mean very much if you have to spend it alone. If you ignored your social life and your friends for year while you built your empire or career, you may find yourself entering retirement with no friends, no family and no one to have fun with in your later years. If you are really rich you might have friends but they might be more friends with your money than with you. Is that your definition of success? For most people this doesn't even come close to what their vision of success is.

Money and careers are important. But so is your health. Long hours of work, increased stress and high workloads all contribute to health related issues like high blood pressure, heart attacks and disease. Fatigue and stress lower the effectiveness of our immune system which helps protect us from the germs and disease that is present all around us.

A balanced lifestyle is a less stressful lifestyle. It allows our bodies to heal, rejuvenate itself and protect us from our environment.

It allows us to relax and recharge our batteries. It also allows us to interact with others and even, wait for this one, laugh a bit once in a while!

Life can be tough at times and sometimes things seem to come at us from every angle and all at the same time. But when we have others to lean on and when we are healthy and vibrant and full of energy, we are much more able to deal with those things. We can shrug them off our back instead of letting them best us down. We can deal more from strength than from weakness.

The question now become not whether we should lead a balanced lifestyle but instead how can we best create that balanced lifestyle. Well, I'm glad you asked because here are a few pointers to help you live happier, healthier and with less stress:

Carve Out Time for Yourself

Everyone needs a little "me" time. We need time to just relax and be alone or in a quiet place. It doesn't matter what we do with that time as much as it matters that we have that time. Read a book, watch TV, go to a movie or just take a nap if you want. The only rule must be that work must never enter your "me" time. You don't do any work, you don't think of any work and you turn off the damned phone too!

Turn Off Your Phone!

30 years ago cell phones were not a part of everyone's life. That meant we could leave the office and leave work behind for while. That's not true anymore. Everyone has a cell phone which means everyone can be contacted almost 24 hours a day 7 days a week. Business calls and texts can come in all times of the day and night. That means we never truly get away from work or business.

We need to cut the imaginary cord at times and either leave the phone home or turn it off all together. Unless you are a doctor or surgeon, chances are no really serious emergency is going to occur overnight or while you are at dinner. If you know something might happen that's important, keep it on that day. Otherwise, when you go to the movies or out to dinner, turn the damned phone off. You will appreciate the peace and quiet and those around you will as well!

Include Family into Your Schedule

OK, I admit it. Sometimes family can be one giant pain in the butt. But they can also be a great influence and source of comfort to you in life. These are the people who usually know you the best and who love you for who you are and w=not what you have become. Family might be your only source for unconditional love so don't ignore them or relegate them to the back of your life.

Make plans to have a dinner together or spend some time together outside of the holidays. Have a bar-b-que I the summer or just get together for the fun of it. Some family members are not going to be around forever so take the opportunity to spend time with them now while you have the chance. If you wait until it is too late, those regrets will stay with you for the rest of your life.

Create a Schedule & Plan

Sometimes life gets so crazy and complicated that we lose sight of what we are doing and how we are doing it. Get yourself a daily pa=lanner and schedule some time for yourself and others in your life and stick to that schedule whenever possible. Block out that time first so it's always there. If you wait until you see what time is left over for the week, you may never get any time at all.

It might help as well to share that schedule with others so they are aware of what you are doing so they do not make commitments for you that might place that set aside time in jeopardy. Anything you can do to protect that time will be helpful. If you have a secretary or a business partner they should absolutely be provided with your time off schedule.

Work Hard but Play Hard too!

Everyone who works hard should play hard too! Make sure you set aside some time to do some stress reduction exercise and have some fun. Join a basketball or volleyball team. Play adult softball or some other sport. Not only does this help you relax, it reduces stress and helps keep you in shape and healthy! Studies have shown that regular exercise makes you more alert and productive as well. So when you take time to play you help yourself and those around you!

Set Aside Time for Special People

One percenters and other successful people understand how important it is to have a special person in their lives to share their success with. Having someone with you to share the ups and downs makes success sweeter and helps you deal with the curveballs that come at us throughout life.

But we need to understand that in order for people to remain in a good relationship that both people have to work together. That means both people have to make themselves available and share things with each other. If one person is obsessed with their career or their job the other person is bound to feel neglected and hurt.

Schedule at least one night a week to spend with each other. Do it more often if you can but it should be one night per week minimum

Do something special on that one night. Go to the movies or out to dinner. Don't just sit and watch sports on TV. Take time to talk with each other and share what is going on in your life. If you have been really busy lately, share the reasons why. Reassure each other of their importance in your life.

If you neglect to do that you might very well come home to an empty house or apartment one day and by that time it is going to be too late. Don't wait until it's too late. Tell then and show them you care right now!

Focus on what is Right for YOU not what's right for Someone Else!

When it comes to how you live your life, only you really know what's important for you. Your family doesn't know what's really inside you and friends don't know either. You have to act according to what's in your heart and soul. You have to live YOUR definition of life and not someone else's.

One of the most stressful things you can do is try and live the life someone else designs for you. Listen to their advice; consider what they have said and then move in the direction that you feel is right for you. You can consult professionals and career counselors and others who are knowledgeable in certain areas but the final decision MUST always be yours!

Take a Damned Vacation!

Here is another area where most people get it absolutely 100% wrong! Everyone needs a vacation every now and then. You don't have to go to a tropical island or someplace expensive. But everyone needs to get away from their routine and their everyday problems and worries. They need to leave business and responsibilities behind and just relax and enjoy themselves.

But a lot of people feel that vacations are a waste of time and that they take them away from growing their business, growing their career or doing whatever they do to increase their income. Some even believe that they are the only ones who can run their business or perform their job function at an acceptable level. In other words, they feel the world will come to an end if they are not around. Well, let me be the first to day that if that is how you look at your place in this world that it's time for a reality check.

There are very few people in this world that cannot be replaced for a short period of time. Even the President of the United States takes a few days off for some rest and relaxation once in a while. As far as the rest of us are concerned our businesses and our jobs will perform just fine while we are away. The only exception might be a business where you are the only employee in an extremely skilled industry but even then there are options.

Doctors and dentists have arrangements with other doctors and dentist to cover for them while they take time off. Partners cover for other partners and employees are usually cross trained to some extent to cover when people are on vacation or sick.

Sick??? Did someone mention being sick? What happens when you are sick? Does your business collapse and slide into oblivion? Does your company stock dive into the toilet when you take a day or a week off? Probably not. In fact, whether or not you like to believe it or not, life will go on just fine as long as you take a few precautions.

Every company and every businessman should have a fall back plan for when they are away for any reason. Whether it's because of sickness, vacation, taking a class or for any reason, these absences occur and you have to learn how to deal with them.

So if you are truly indispensible and that no one can possibly do what you do, you need to come up with a backup plan to carry on while you are away. Everyone needs to have a backup plan and you do as well.

But getting back to vacations, these are not only important to give your mind and body a break from the daily stresses and problems; they are a way to get back in touch with others in your life. They give you a chance to spend time with family and friends and recharge your batteries.

This is important for both emotional and health reasons. When you feel good you perform better and when you are happier you are able to accomplish more.

Listen to Your "Inner Voice"

We have said this many times already but your body and your mind are very good at letting us know when they need something. They let us know when they are tired or stressed or when things get a little much. Do not ignore these signals.

If you are tired, get some rest. If you sick, make the time to get back to health. Successful people understand they can only be their best when they feel their best. They also understand that they have just one body for their entire lives. While science and health care can help us keep it healthy, they cannot keep us from experiencing the effects of abuse. It's never too late to start treating our mind and body better. It is never too late to create balance and correct bad habits that created problem in our lives.

Summary

Always look at life as several things that are combined into one. Make an effort to pay attention to and attend to all parts of your life. Carve out time for yourself, family and friends. Spend time on business and career growth and improving yourself but leave time for a vibrant social life as well.

Also, understand there is value in doing absolutely nothing at times. Spending a day just recharging your batteries and preparing yourself for the week ahead is not being lazy. It is being smart. So let's be smart, let's live smart and let's start creating balance throughout your life.

Let's start right now!

Cutting Down on Distractions & Wasted Time

If there is one thing that separates the rest of us from the one percenters and other successful people it is the way we use our time. As we stated before in this book, everyone gets the same 24 hours in a day. No one gets any more or any less. So it is important that we use our time to the very best of our ability. Two ways we can do that are to reduce wasted time and eliminate or at least control distractions that keep us from doing the things we should be doing.

Let's first talk about distractions a little bit. We all have them and we cannot eliminate them. They take on several different forms and there are some of them we might not even realize exist until we stop and think about them.

What are the things that distract you from doing the things you need to do in life or work? Do people interrupt you? Are you a slave to e-mail or voice mail? Is your phone more of a hindrance to you than it is a tool?

These are just a few of the most common distractions everyone has to deal with in their lives and their jobs. More time is spent dealing with distractions than any other situation that might keep us from getting things done. Distractions interrupt our work flow, derail our train of thought, and keep us from completing tasks as quickly and we could.

Successful people have distractions like the rest of us but they refuse to allow them to dictate how they go through their normal day. Instead they control their distractions and deal with them on their own terms. You cannot eliminate most distractions so you have to design processes and procedures that allow you to integrate these distractions into your life as painlessly as possible.

Here are some of the most common distractions and what you can do to enable yourself to have more time to get more done:

Telephone Calls

The telephone is a great tool for us in life. It allows us to talk to a lot of people in a short time and allows us to be more productive as well. But it also can be one of the greatest distractions we have on a daily basis.

Phone calls interrupt our train of thought and the flow of our work. We have to stop doing what we are doing and change what we are thinking about whenever we have to answer the phone. With so many people having a greater and easier access to telephones these days, these interruptions can cost us hours and hours of lost time every week.

There are a few ways we can deal with telephone interruptions. One way is to simply take the phone off the hook but this might conflict with company policies as well as risking the importance of missing a really critical call. If there is something you need to do for a few minutes, this approach will work. But if it is for a longer period of time then we will have to move on to idea #2

This works extremely well for most people. Restrict your use of the phone during specific periods of the day. Let's say you will answer your phone or listen to messages from 8AM to 9AM, then again from 12PM to 1PM and again at 4PM. This will give you time to receive calls and check messages while giving you blocks of 3 hours where you can work uninterrupted. That means you now have 6 hours of uninterrupted time per day! Naturally this will depend on the nature of your business but checking your phone every 3 hours is not unreasonable for most of us. You should update your message to let people know when they should expect a reply.

Another method that works if you work in an office is to let someone else answer your phone for a certain period of time. If you have a secretary, have your secretary screen your calls and tell most people you are unavailable and then take a message. If there is no secretary, switch off with someone else in the office when you need "quiet" time. You can answer another person's calls when they need quiet time.

As a last resort, and you should do this only when you are up against the wall on a project or close deadline, have voicemail take all your calls and have a message letting people know you will be out of the office until tomorrow. Then, monitor your messages and leave the replies to non critical calls for tomorrow. If any calls are very important, return those calls today. No one ever complained that someone called back before they said they would!

Cell Phone / Text Messages

I am one of those people who absolutely hates cell phones. Yes, they are great when you get a flat tire out in the middle of nowhere but for everyday use, they are one heck of a distraction! People who have access 24 hours a day whenever and wherever they might be find it way too easy to call you for any number of reasons.

They call you from the grocery store or while sitting in the waiting room at the doctors. I guess their feeling is that they have time to waste so you probably do too!

Add to that the constant barrage of texts and other information and you wind up with a colossal waste of time reading and responding to all these calls and messages. If you are going to remain productive, you have to be able to control your cell phone and how you use it in life.

The mute button on your cell phone ringer is a wonderful thing. Place your phone in silent mode so you won't hear it if is rings. Take off the vibrate feature as well so you won't hear it ring or signal a text. Then, put the phone in another place where you can't see it or at least turn it over so you won't see the face of the phone as new texts or messages come through. If you know something came across curiosity will force you to check it out.

Another option your phone might have is to receive e-mails as well. This can either be a great help or a great nuisance. If you absolutely have to be able to read e-mails away from the office or when you are not home then turn this feature on. If you don't turn it off! You will waste a ton of time reading spam type e-mails and texts!

Another advantage of cell phones is that you can leave them at home, leave them in the car when you enter meetings or just keep them out of sight when you want peace and quiet and uninterrupted time.

Don't be a slave to your cell phone. Use it as a tool but do not let it dictate how you spend your day and how much work you get done. Use it properly but restrict its impact on your life.

E-Mail

When it comes to time wasters, e-mail is way up there. There is no cost for sending e-mails so companies send out millions of these e-mails and people spend thousands of hours reading this garbage. Fortunately there are a few easy things we can do to limit the effects of reading e-mails.

First, designate specific times for reading and answering e-mails. Usually first thing in the morning and the last hour of the day are the best times. This was you handle things first thing in the morning and also before you leave for the day. This will free up more time during the day to work on projects, report and other assignments.

Second, learn how to assign your e-mails into groups. Create folders for your e-mails and then when you have a bunch of e-mails file them into separate folders. Create a folder named "important" and put important e-mails in that folder. Create a "spam" or "shopping" folder and put those e-mails in that folder. Lastly create a "personal" folder and store your personal or private e-mails in that folder.

This will take just a few minutes but you will then be able to focus your efforts on the e-mails that really matter until you have free time to handle the rest of them.

Stop e-mail abuse at the root by not giving out your personal or work e-mail to anyone or any website you don't know personally. This will keep you off spam lists and commercial type e-mails. You can use one of the free e-mail services available on line for all these other types of e-mails. You can check out those e-mails whenever you have the opportunity or desire to do so.

Internet

Studies have shown that many businesses lose hours and hours of supposed work time by people surfing the internet. They do shopping, watch videos, listening to music, surf for information and other non business related tasks. Many companies restrict internet access for that very reason.

The problem with surfing the internet is that time can just fly by without you realizing how long you have been at it. You look at the clock and discover you have been on line for two hours and it seems like 5 minutes!

Keep off the internet at all times unless there is a business reason to be online. Otherwise you will find yourself wasting a lot of time that could have been better spent getting business related activities completed.

Save your surfing for home or your lunch break!

Interruptions

I love working at home because I have no interruptions. People do not stop by my desk asking me if I want to go to lunch or telling me their jokes or letting me know how some party went over the weekend. It's not that I am anti-social, it's just that I have work to do and do not need these interruptions keeping me from what I am doing.

If you work in an office and you need some quiet time, see if there is someplace quiet you can go to do your work. Maybe there is a vacant office or even a storeroom you might use. Perhaps you could come in early or stay late to take advantage of some office quiet time.

If the problem because severe, you might not have any chance but to tell people you have work to do and not to bother you during the day. But if you take such drastic action you should be aware that it might turn people against you and label you a snob or as anti-social.

Have Self Discipline

So far we have blamed everyone and everything else for causing distractions in our lives.

While there are a ton of distractions caused by other people and other things, some of our distractions come from another source. They come directly from us.

If you are easily distracted, that can present a problem. If you find yourself constantly stopping to read a book or a magazine or doing other things because you don't really want to work, that is all on you. If that is the case, then you have a few environmental issues to take care of.

If there are things in your work area or in the workplace that distract you or tempt you, get rid of them. Place books and magazine out of sight or get rid of them all together. If music is a distraction, turn off the radio or the office sound system. If you have any electronic gadgets or games, bring them home. Whatever causes you to lose focus needs to be removed from your work area.

Wasted Time

Do you waste a lot of time? Do you take longer to get things done than anyone else? If you do, then perhaps you waste time doing things the wrong way or in the wrong order. If that is the case, here are some tips to help you get straightened out.

Be Orderly

It pays to take the time to do things in the right order.

Always do things that need to be done first before you attempt to do other things. We discussed this in another chapter of this book. This results in fewer work stoppages and a much more efficient work flow.

Be Organized

This is something else we already discussed in this book. Knowing where everything is and having everything you need at your fingertips will enable you to spend less time searching for something and then use that time to get more accomplished. The more convenient things are to use the more likely we are to use them. So not only do we get more done in less time, our results are usually much better at the same time!

Do Things Right the First Time?

Whenever you have to do something over a second or third time that is wasted time. Spend a little extra time the first time so that you do it right. This will eliminate duplication of efforts which saves time and resources. Never feel it is acceptable to do things multiple times if you could do it just once with the same results.

Be Flexible

We all have schedules and things we plan to get accomplished.

If our schedule gets disturbed because of something that popped up at the last minute, we need to be able to "plug in" alternative tasks or assignments to make use of that time we had dedicated to something else. For example, if we planned to work on our quarterly report all day today but the information we need is delayed until tomorrow, we should have others tasks or assignments ready to do today. We should not use the opportunity to take a 4 hours lunch or read magazines all day.

The ability to be flexible and to be ready to adapt to anything that comes our way is one way to set yourself apart from everyone else. Never let distraction interrupt your focus on being productive!

Outsourcing

One of the most important things that set apart the one percenters from the rest of the crowd is their ability to get more done in less time. One of the ways they do this is by leveraging the skills and talents of others to help them get things done faster. There are several advantages to this and a few cautions as well. In this chapter we will discuss the pro-s and cons regarding outsourcing.

For those who are not aware, outsourcing is the term used when you hire or have an arrangement with other people to provide goods or services to you or your clients and customers. People often do this when they either do not have the particular skills or expertise to do something themselves or they don't have the time to do those things themselves.

Outsourcing is a powerful tool because it allows you to have several things being done at the same time usually by people who have a higher level of skill or expertise than you do. That is not something to be ashamed of nor should you feel weaker for realizing other people can do some things better than you can.

Actually, it is an indication of extreme self confidence on your part. You understand that getting something done right and getting it done faster is important to you and your company or business. Results matter more than who does the work that produces them. After all would you like to make $50,000 doing something yourself or $250,000 having someone else do it that does it better and brings in more sales?

Outsourcing is also valuable in the beginning of our career or when we start a business because it allows us to "rent" expertise instead of bringing in partners or employees. This saves you money and reduces overhead. That can be critical especially in the start-up phase.

But since outsourcing is also something that could possibly have a downside for you, here are some of the pro-s and cons to using outsourcing:

Pros:

Instant Expertise

If you are need something done that you are not really skilled or prepared to do, then you either have to hire someone with those particular skills or find a consultant. Both can take time to get on board and both are usually costly options. But if you can find someone who you can outsource something to on a job by job basis, you can add that expertise to your list as something you can offer.

When a business or career is just getting started, this can be a great way to create more and better products or offer better and more impressive services. This way if a client asks you if you can provide a certain area of expertise, you can say YES! And not risk losing that client to someone else.

Get Things Done Faster

It just makes sense that if you outsource 4 tasks to others then you and those 4 other people can work on 5 things at the same time! That means moving forward faster, delivering products or services faster and even being able to handle multiple clients and projects at the same time!

Not only that but it might take you 2 or 3 times longer to do the same exact task than it does for someone more skilled that has more experience. Anyone who has tried to slog through an Excel spreadsheet with no experience will know what I am talking about! More skill let's people do things faster than you ever would.

This is one of the main benefits of outsourcing, the ability to get products and service developed and onto the shelves faster, the ability to provide faster responses to customers and to get projects done well within their deadlines are just some of the advantages of outsourcing.

Get Things Done Better

You have heard the expression: "jack of all trades and master of none". That means most of us try and do everything ourselves instead of concentrating on the things we can do best. So we can do 20 things "OK" but none of them really well.

The result is our results are OK but not that great. You might be able to create a basic graphic in Photoshop but a professional will create the same type of graphic and it will knock your eyes out. Yours will just be "OK".

If you remember other parts of this book we talk about always looking to produce the best results because everything is a competition and the best results usually wind up getting most of the opportunities. So if someone else can do something better, and it's an important situation, go with the person who will get the best results!

You Get to Do What You Do Best!

When we spend our time doing what we do best, we create the best value for our company or business and also ourselves. An added benefit is that we get to do more of what we enjoy and that's always a good thing as well!

Let's say that your strength is wring advertising copy. If you outsource your web design and packaging tasks and use that time to write 4 really good ads or brochures that is time better spent than spending time designing boxes or packing orders. You can generate more revenue and business writing advertising copy than doing those other tasks. You will usually find the most successful people and business utilize people by allowing them to do the things each of them does best. This is the way to maximize value and productivity while keeping people happy at the same time.

It's Usually Cheaper

Outsourcers are paid only when you give them a job or when you need them. If you don't need them, you don't have to pay them. The same cannot be said for an employee. If you don't need an employee for a week or a month, you still have to pay their salary and benefits. With an outsourcer you don't.

Now you have to understand that you will probably have to pay them more per hour than an employee because they have to live and they need medical care and other benefits as well but they have to bear the cost. So expect to pay a little more quality results. This will not always be the case but be prepared for it.

Faster Growth

Start-up companies and single people are usually up against considerable obstacles when they first start out. They cannot be expected to match the manpower and resources of larger, more established firms or companies yet that's what clients need and expect. So outsourcing can come in handy to provide additional man power and expertise when needed.

You are then able to offer more types of service, more areas of expertise and other benefits usually only available from the bigger firms or companies. As you grow and find a constant need for a certain service or area of expertise, you can actually hire an employee for that position. But for now, outsourcing can be a great help.

Evaluation of Future Partners or Employees

Outsourcing can be a great way to see how someone does when assigned tasks.

For example, if you have an outsourcer who is really great at graphic design and produces some awesome results, when you are ready to hire a graphic designer you already have someone in mind! Many people start out with outsourcing either to supplement their income or find full time work. Either way, it's a win-win for everyone!

Good for Infrequent Needs

As we said before, if you need a certain type of expertise once or twice a year, it doesn't pay to invest in a permanent employee. In those cases, you find a reliable outsourcer who can step in and perform those tasks for you on a per job basis.

You might even want to place that person on some kind of retainer arrangement where they earn slightly more in exchange for making themselves available to you when they are needed. Steady and repeat work is the goal of every outsourcer or consultant.

Cons

We mentioned the most common reasons why outsourcing can really help you and your business. But few things in life are 100% positive and outsourcing is no different. Here are a few things you should be aware of when considering outsourcing for your particular needs:

Security / Theft

If you are developing new or exclusive and you are afraid of someone stealing or copying your idea, then outsourcing might not be the best path for you to take. Any time you let someone else see what you are doing you run the risk of them taking your idea and copying it or even selling it to others. You then find your product or idea on the shelves before yours is even ready. While you can make people sign confidentiality forms, those can be difficult and expensive to enforce.

Quality Concerns

Whenever you do something personally, or when an employee you know does something, you have a pretty good idea what kind of result you are going to get. You know the quality of the work that you and others you know are capable of. When you hire an outsourcer, all of that vanishes.

You can (and should) ask for samples of their work and a few references but sometimes those are fake or misrepresented. I always recommend trying out an outsourcer on some little project, maybe even a "phony" one just to see what kind of result you get. If it is a good result then go with that person. If the results are poor, look for someone else.

Reputation Concerns

This is probably the most important thing to remember when it comes to outsourcing. Your clients or other people who ask you for something are going to hold YOU accountable even if the work is being done by someone else. Your name is on the letterhead or on the front door and everything that is done by your business reflects on you.

If an outsourcer does a bad job, or provides inaccurate information, that is going to reflect bad on you not the outsourcer. Usually outsourcers work behind the lines and anonymously. Only you know who did the work. You have to be prepared to accept the responsibility for everything produced by your company or business whether you did the work or someone else.

Loss of Total Control

When you do something yourself, you have total control over how it's done and when it's done. You control the quality and the materials used and how everything proceeds. When you hire outside people to do the work, you lose a certain amount of control.

You will find yourself relying on other people to adhere to deadlines and to produce a certain quality of work. Usually you are not standing over them as they work. You will give them a task or assignment and a deadline and then hope they finish on time.

If they do, that's great. But if they get sick, find a higher paying assignment, or just don't feel like doing your work anymore, you might find yourself in trouble.

That is why you should build in extra time into anything that is being done by an outsourcer. No one gets upset if something is done ahead of schedule so add some time to make sure things will be done when you need them.

Where Do You Find Outsourcers?

There are many places you can find outsourcers both online and locally. Just do a search online and you will be taken to various sites that provide both types of services. Local Yellow Page and other publications might be of help as well.

But the best way to find the best people is through personal recommendation or word of mouth. Using the same people that other people are very satisfied with will make your chances of finding someone good much better.

What Should I Pay?

How much someone is going to charge you is going to depend greatly on the type of task, what kind of skill or expertise is involved and how long the task is likely to take.

For example, paying someone to create a graphic for you might cost you only $5 - $10 online. But if you need someone to meet with a client and prepare a safety evacuation plan that meets local building codes that could cost you $1,000's!

One thing I will say is that you will usually get what you pay for. If you look at 10 outsourcers and all of them want $100 to do the task while one wants $10, then I would really wonder why that one person only wants $10. Any time someone quotes you a price that is way off from the rest of the outsourcers, wonder why that is.

Higher might be because the person spends extra time and does a better job than everyone else. Or, they just might feel their work is worth more when it's really not. Investigate, check with references and make sure you get the right value for your money.

What Should I know Before Hiring an Outsourcer?

Would you buy a car without knowing how much it costs? Would you buy a product if you didn't know what it did or how well it did it? Of course you wouldn't and you should approach hiring an outsourcer the same way.

People are out to make as much money as they can and they thrive on people who know little or nothing about what they are asking them to do. If something should take 2 hours and you can convince them it will take you 6 hours, then you make more money. It's just common sense.

Before hiring someone to do anything for you it should be standard practice to have a working knowledge of what is involved in completing that task. Then you can talk intelligently to the outsourcer using any applicable technical or industry terms and let them know you are not a fool and will not be easy to trick or over charge.

Also, have some idea of what it would cost to sub contract this type of task to someone else. If you get 2 o3 prices you have a rough idea what should be charged. Look online, get a few estimates and only then make your decision.

Check references and reviews if available before hiring someone. Be careful with online reviews because some people use other names and give themselves amazing reviews. Spend some time upfront trying to find the right person.

When Should I stay Away from Outsourcing?

While sometimes we have no choice when it comes to using outside help to assist us, there will be times when we could use outsourcing but shouldn't. This will not occur all that often and when you find really good and reliable outsourcers these situations may come up even less frequently. But here are a few times when you should consider keeping things in-house:

When the Situation is High Profile

If you have a really high profile or valuable job or critical task, ask yourself in your interests are best served turning that over to someone else. Though they might do the job faster, will they do it better? Will you be able to present the results to your client and understand what the results mean and how they were compiled?

Is the job going to represent a huge opportunity for you or your company? Will it have high visibility to other people? If the answer to either of those questions is yes, then consider doing most of the work yourself so you will have the opportunity to add the little touches that just might make all the difference in the world.

Jobs or assignments that are critical to your career or business growth often benefit by actual hands on efforts from someone who has something on the line.

For an outsourcer, your job might be one of many they are working on. They know they will get paid when they are finished so they might rush through it, do a good job but not a great one, and then send it to you so you get paid.

Do You Understand What Needs to be Done & How It's Done?

You are responsible for everything you present to your client or to your boss. Your reputation hinges on the quality of work you produce as well as your understanding of that work and how it was done. The last thing you want or need is to have someone ask you a question about something you or your company did and you don't have the answer. That is why before you hire any outsourcer you should have a working knowledge of what is to be done, who it is done and how long it should take. Then as questions are asked, you will be able to intelligently answer them.

When the Situation is Sensitive

As we said before, if you have a new idea or concept that you are looking to develop, you might seriously want to keep everything under wraps and not share it with anyone else. If the value of your product or idea is very high, I would think twice about getting anyone else exposed to it.

Always remember there are people out there who are not anywhere near as honest as you or I!

When there are Legal Issues Involved

This can be a tough one. If you are involved in anything the law or legal requirements are part of the task or assignment, be very careful about trusting the task to someone from outside. If you do hire someone you will have to make sure that they are aware of the local codes, laws, regulations and other issues that might vary widely from area to area.

A general rule might be that the more legal exposure you might have, the more you should either keep it in house or hire a local expert to do the task for you. Always remember that it is your name on the front door or on the letterhead so you are responsible. While you might be able to turn around and take legal action on the outsourcer, that can get time consuming and expensive. It can also become a logistical nightmare if the person is located in another state or another country. Just be careful.

Do You Have Commitment Issues?

When it comes to being successful, whether you make it to one percenter status or not, you have to be committed to the entire process. Commitment is something that a lot of people just are not willing to do these days. They want the benefits and everything that goes with them but they are not committed to the process it takes to get to that point.

Instead, for a reason evidently only known and understood by a few sacred souls, people today seem to think they are entitled to stuff. Even if they do not work for it or do anything whatsoever to earn it. I'm not one of the people who understand this attitude and quite frankly, I'm proud of that.

Successful people understand that success is not a right or a privilege and it definitely is not something people are entitled to.

Success, like respect and honor, is earned. You do what it takes to achieve your goals and move forward in this world. Those that are willing to do that become successful. Those who are unwilling to do that rely on being lucky and winning the lottery.

Throughout this book we have explained character traits and attitudes that are necessary for building long term growth and success. These are designed not to make you one of the rest but instead, turn you into one of the best. You don't have to do all of them as some of them might not really apply to you. But you must make a commitment to yourself to do what it takes to get where you want in life.

The bad news is that the commitment we are talking about is not for a year or 2 or even five or ten years, it is pretty much a lifelong commitment. Attitudes are usually not turned on and off like a faucet. We adopt a way of thinking and acting and it follows us throughout our lives. For most of us, the hardest part is getting started. Once we get started, we usually are motivated by our success as we go through life. It is that first step that stops many of us dead in our tracks.

The good news is that virtually everything we talk about in this book can be done by anyone and I mean anyone. Attitudes require determination and practice until they turn into habits. Honesty does not require a college education or a huge bank account.

If you have the right attitude and you go through life in an honest manner, you will get further in life. There is no magic solution or magic potion. You can do this, your neighbor can do this and most of your co-workers can do this. (I say most because there is always at least one clueless co-worker. The same applies to brother-in-laws as well.)

But commitment does require work, especially at first. You have to be committed to giving your best effort in everything you do. Not some of the things you do and not half the things you do. Everything. You need to train your mind that being good enough is just not going to be good enough. You need to train yourself to be the best, do your best and act like you're the best.

It might be difficult at first. It is hard to act like something you don't really believe that you are. But as time goes by and as you do more and more things better, you will come to believe that you are among the best. The one day you have a revelation and all of this becomes clear to you and you believe.

Success and wealth comes over time and you grow and become more valuable and knowledgeable. It does not happen overnight and it doesn't happen in a month or a year. Yes, you will make progress but this happens over extended periods of time. It requires effort, it requires patience and it requires commitment.

Commitment is not a difficult concept to understand. People who commit themselves to a cause or a process become successful more often than those who don't. That's just the way things go. You need to believe that and tell yourself that starting today you are going to do what it takes to get you where you want to be.

Commitment and belief are what takes less skilled and talented people past those with more natural ability. Given a choice between an entitled person and a hard working but lesser talented person and I will take the hard worker every time. These are the people who believe in the concept of hard work and determination. I need you to become one of those people right now.

So now I have some questions for you.

Are you going to commit to the entire process?

Are you going to refuse to be satisfied with anything less than your best?

Are you going to be the one who pushes on when others give up?

Are you going to be the one that turns failure into success?

Are you going to be the one who looks back and smiles with no regrets or are you going to look back and wish you had been more serious about things in the beginning?

Make the commitment today. Take the first step today and then take at least one other step each and every day. Never stop and never waver. Always move forward even if the step you take is a tiny one. Become the person you know you can be.

You can do it. I know you can. All you need is some commitment.

A Love Story

We saved two of the most important parts for the last two chapters of the book. While this is not absolutely positively required, really enjoying and loving what you do can make all the difference in the world to you as you go through life.

Most successful people, and many one percenters, became that way because they turned their passions into their careers or businesses. By doing so, they got to do what most people only get to dream about. They get to earn a living doing something they love to do. So the argument can be made that they will never really work a day in their lives!

Doing something you love is good for other reasons as well. You usually give a better effort because you are doing things you like and you are doing them because they are your passion. You are not content with doing things like other people do.

You want to do things in new and different ways that fuel your passion for what you love!

We just finished talking about commitment and that's another area where doing something you love comes into play. How much commitment do you really need to continue to do something you love? Not much I am sure. It takes commitment to stay on your diet but it doesn't take much commitment at all to eat filet mignon on a regular basis. When you are doing something you love doing it is not a sacrifice, it is rewarding and fun.

So if you are just starting out, or if a career change is on your horizon, do yourself a huge favor. Try and choose something you really love and enjoy. Almost any passion can be turned into a thriving business or career if you think it through.

Don't get trapped into doing something just for the money. Money is a temporary motivator at best. Once you have money and get used to it, the boredom and frustration of doing something you don't like will return. That's what happens when you do something for all the wrong reasons.

So don't choose your business or career based on the wrong reasons. Instead, choose something for the right reasons. Do something you love and never work another day in your life!

The One Percenter Golden Rule

NOTE: You will notice that some of this has already been covered throughout this book but we wanted to bring it all together in one place and discuss it in the proper context. In any case, this can be so important it deserves to be covered twice!

We always like to save something important or special for the last chapter in all our books. In this case, we'd like to end with something that is so basic and important that we sometimes forget just how critical this simple concept really is.

How we treat other people has a direct impact on how they treat us and interact with us. In a world where opportunities sometimes are scarce, we need other people to help us throughout our lives. We need friends, partners, associates and people willing to help us. In other words, we want to develop strong relationships with the people we meet.

We also mentioned several times throughout this book that life and business are actually competitions with the winner getting the new job or getting the best opportunities. Like it or not, how we treat other people will have a definite impact on how successful we become.

While ever competition has just one winner, how that person wins and how they react to winning makes a big difference. People respect other people who win honestly and handle their success with dignity and respect. They do not respect people who get to the top by stepping on people on their way.

One percenters realize that they need other people, and the relationships they have with those people in order to become more successful. No one makes it through life alone and you are no exception. If you win something at the expense of a relationship the cost of that win was probably too great.

Here are some things you should always consider when it comes to how you treat other people:

The Golden Rule

Most of us know the golden rule "Treat others like you would like them to treat you". For most of us, this is a very simple way to go through life and treat people properly. Ask yourself if you would like to be treated they exact same way that you treat others in your life.

If the answer is yes, and you are being honest, that's a great start!

It is important that you realize that customers, co-workers, management and clients deep down are people just like you and I. They want the same basic things in life that you and I want. They want to be happy, feel appreciated and they want to be treated with dignity and respect. If you can provide that kind of treatment, your chances of forming long lasting relationships will be much greater.

Always Look for the Win-Win

People like to get as much of what they want as possible. Everyone is like that. People who go through life trying to give others as much of what they want often go much further in life and in business. Even though we have stated many times that life is a competition that does not mean that everything is a "to the death" fight with just one clear cut winner who gets everything.

The "winner take all" attitude is not one that will get you very far. It might get you some short term gains but over the long haul, it will hurt you. No one likes to be bullied, cheated or taken advantage of in the process of doing business. Those who resort to those kinds of tactics usually do business with someone once and that's it. People who were, or feel they were, victimized usually will stay clear of that person for a very long time.

Instead, try and arrive at solutions or resolutions that give all parties the most of what they need or want as possible. If you need to resolve a problem, do it in such a way that enables you to get a fair result while giving the other person or company some of what they expected as well. Be fair. Do not go for the throat every time you try to get something.

Always Consider the Other Person

All too often we find ourselves thinking about what we need out of a situation and ignoring the needs of the other person. This not uncommon because human nature is to think of what we want and need as opposed to what the other people need. But if we put ourselves in the place of the other person, we often get a new dimension to the situation.

When we look at something through the eyes of the other person, we get insight into the problem from their point of view. We see their needs and the reasons behind them. We get a much better idea of the emotions behind their words as well. Even more important, we often discover ways of making everyone happy by creating solutions that address the needs of everyone.

If you can manage to do this on a regular basis you will develop a very positive reputation for being honest and fair. A reputation like that can be a powerful ally for you moving forward in life.

People will come to you first because they know you will be fair with them and give them more of what they need than other people.

Treat People with Dignity & Respect

People deserve to be treated with dignity and respect. Even if you don't respect a person for things they have done or said, you should treat them with respect anyway. You should not go down to their level and respond in the same manner they behave.

You can disagree with people without getting nasty and offensive. Though many people resort to that kind of behavior, it does not have a positive effect on the relationship. The most beneficial conversations occur when both people are calm and in control. Think about the last time someone yelled and cursed at you. Did you really want to do your best to help them? Probably not. For me personally, I will go out of my way for someone who treats me well and is understanding. For the others, not so much!

That means using the right type of language and not saying or doing anything that would offend someone or make them feel bad about themselves. Just as we stated in the last item, if you take the time to put yourself in the place of the other person, you can choose your words and approach much more accurately.

Don't Take Advantage of Others

No one likes to be cheated or taken advantage of. If you have to resort to those kinds of tactics to get what you want in life you need to re-evaluate your career choice. Very few people make it to the top and stay there by lying and cheating people or taking advantage of people on a regular basis. They might get some short term gains but they will eventually fall and the fall will be swift and severe.

I am not talking about using your competitive advantage to land a deal or get a job. If you are the best person or company for the job you should say so in order to land that job. But if you have to slam someone else or take credit for work you have not done, that will come back to haunt you.

There will also come certain times where people are extremely vulnerable and might have to do things they normally would never consider. Maybe they are in financial chaos and are forced to sell something to pay off the debt. If you find yourself in such a situation, take the high road and pay a fair price. It doesn't have to be full price because you should want to get a good deal as well. But offer a fair price and do not take advantage of people when they are down.

I realize that this is how a lot of business is done and I must say that saddens me.

But I have also seen people who have stepped up and given the other person a better deal than they might have received and that has paid off handsomely for them in the future. It's all about reputation and how you treat others. The cream always comes to the top and that's exactly where you want to be.

Climb the Ladder with Integrity

We mentioned this before and it bears repeating. As you go through your career and try to get a better job or grow your business do NOT try and do it by putting down others or stepping on their backs in the process.

Earn your way to the top with ethical values and behavior. Get that new job by being the best candidate not by making everyone else look bad. There is so much of this going on today and you should always try to be a part of it. Otherwise you may find yourself all alone at the top with no one having your back. Or maybe they have your back but there's a huge target on it!

Be Honest & Trustworthy

We close this discussion with a basic tenant that we all should live by. That is going through life being honest and trustworthy. Always take the high road and remain honest. It's perfectly fine to be aggressive and go after the things in life that you want. But it's how you go about it that makes all the difference.

There will come a time when you look back over your life and see how far you came and how you got there. When that time comes you want to smile at what you have done and have few regrets. We all make mistakes from time to time and that's fine. But your overall approach should be one of honesty and trustworthiness.

Conclusion

We have come a long way throughout this book and we have covered some very important and some very basic topics and concepts. I hope you learned a lot in this book and also hope that some of the content in these pages helped you to see things just a little bit differently. Because sometimes all we need is a different perspective in order to make a huge difference in our lives.

I also hope that you see the importance of making right decisions and to think long term instead of just what you are doing today. Smart and successful people are able to do that and this is one of the reasons they are so smart and successful.

We also hope that you understand that success is mostly a state of mind. It's what you want in life and for some people it has nothing to do with money or financial gain. It's all about what your love in life and what makes you happy.

But that doesn't mean wanting more money and the things that go along with it is bad or somehow wrong. You should always go after what you want in life as long as you go about it in the right way. Don't take shortcuts and do not get your success at the expense of someone else.

Being a one percenter in anything takes time, commitment and work. But if you truly enjoy what you do, the work part of it disappears and the commitment part just doesn't exist for you. After all, who needs to be committed to something they love doing? They would do it for no other reason than the fact that they love it.

But regardless what success might mean to you, it is important that you focus on your entire life and not just one part. While there may be times when one part of life takes up most of your efforts, always try to return to a balanced life that provides you with everything you need to be happy. When you are able to do that, happiness and success are so much easier to achieve.

So we are at the point where it is time to act. We have come to the point where you have a decision to make. What are you going to do from this point on? What type of person are you going to be in this life? What do you want and how are you going to go about getting it? These are the questions you are going to have to ask yourself in order to move forward towards your goals.

But there is some great news as well. Even though change will be soon entering your life, this is a wonderful point in your life as well. There will be excitement, achievement, happiness and fulfillment waiting for you if you make the right choices and decisions. If you stay the course and make the right choices, you will get to see your life move in directions you never thought possible and you will achieve what you never thought would become your reality.

Make the right choices, do things the right way and you will find yourself looking back over your life and smiling and say "Look what I did and look how I did it!"

And you will smile again and again and again.

www.ingramcontent.com/pod-product-compliance
Lightning Source LLC
Chambersburg PA
CBHW071757200526
45167CB00017B/362